# The Forgotten Bride

*How the Church betrayed its Jewish Heritage*

DAVID LAMBOURN

# DEDICATION

To faithful intercessors around the world who pray night and day
for God's chosen people.

# CONTENTS

# PREFACE

In the British general election of December 2019 the Labour Party plunged into a catastrophic electoral meltdown, achieving its worst performance since 1935. One of the key issues was the degree to which institutional anti-Semitism had taken hold of the party. The previous year one Jewish MP, who later left the party, had been forced to attend Labour's annual conference with a police escort because of the level of verbal attacks made against her.

The problems in the Labour Party, however, are symptoms of a far wider malaise. Despite the British public's heavy punishment of Labour in the 2019 poll, dark forces continue to work behind the scenes. With some noble exceptions, an ingrained antipathy towards the Jewish people has lurked below the surface of many aspects of

British culture and society since the Middle Ages, when they were effectively barred from living in England for over three centuries.

And this is just the tip of a much bigger iceberg. Across the continent of Europe, a deep subliminal prejudice against the Jews has given rise to a harrowing tale of bloodshed, with countless innocent victims being mercilessly butchered over the course of history.

One place that one might hope would be gloriously free from such attitudes is the church of Jesus Christ. However, the hallowed precincts of Christendom are far from innocent in this matter. Even a cursory glance at history would reveal that the church's treatment of the Jews over the centuries has violated everything that Jesus taught, fought for and died for. And so often, where the church has led in its twisted theology, the nations have followed.

Yet somehow we have turned our backs and forgotten. Too many Christians today are ignorant of the poisonous tale of penury, persecutions and pogroms which contaminate the pages of church history, a grim harvest in which murderous seeds of hatred came to sprout and bear abundant fruit. Even today many of these seeds still lie dormant in our churches because we fail to acknowledge their existence.

At the root of this terrible tale lies a question which on the surface appears to be completely innocuous. What is the place of Jewish people in salvation history? In the Old Testament Israel held a unique position among all the nations of the world. No other single nation had been ordained through a direct promise of God. We see Israel described as God's son, his firstborn, and even his beloved.

But do these promises still hold true for the Jewish people today, or have they now been transferred in their entirety to the church, as an increasing proportion of evangelicals appear to believe?[1] Many of us would consider this to be a marginal issue, interesting as a subject of conversation but of no practical consequences for the outworking of our faith, and perhaps an unnecessary distraction from the pressing issues we face as Christians today.

I would strongly disagree. This is a life or death question. The answer we give to this question completely changes the way we read the Bible and the way we understand our place within God's purposes. We simply cannot run away from it. Moreover, it is a matter of the utmost seriousness because together, as participants in church history, as I have already implied, we have blood on our hands.

In the light of this I have expressed myself boldly at times. Some of my statements may occasionally seem rather blunt. The last thing I want to do in this book is to set a judgmental tone or express a partisan and unbalanced opinion. I am only too well aware of how subconscious prejudices, or arrogance about a cherished position, can taint our understanding of scripture and our love for one another. Divisiveness is a cancer that eats away at the body of Christ, and as members of that one body, it is time to stop judging one another and to forgive and embrace each other. However, we do at the same time need to stand together in all our varied traditions and face up to the deadly consequences of our actions in the past.

For this reason I have not held back in attempting to show how together we may have wandered into the most serious error, which inadvertently blighted the lives of millions. My fervent hope, however, even where I may be wrong, is that it will cause the reader to think and reflect on what he or she really believes on this matter and why. My desire is that each of us will emerge with a renewed love for the very people-group to whom Jesus devoted his whole life ministering and which has been scarred by the cruelty of countless generations of our forebears.

This book divides into three broad sections. In the first four chapters we will trace the consequences of what has sometimes been called 'replacement theology' for the church and the Jewish people over the course of history and consider its underlying spiritual roots. In the next four chapters we will look at the arguments drawn from the New Testament that are used to justify viewing the church as the 'new Israel' and consider whether such a standpoint is really defensible. In the final four chapters we will cast our focus back to some recurring themes in the Old Testament, considering what they mean not just for the later struggle between Christianity and Judaism, but also for the troubled relationship between Israel and the Arab world today. We will conclude by assessing the impact which this might have on the current political deadlock in the Middle East.

I owe a small but dedicated group of intercessors in Basingstoke on Friday mornings a great deal in the preparation of this study. While they may not agree with everything I say here, many of them will recognise their own reflections hidden in the material I share. I would like to honour their perseverance, tenacity, and faithfulness, as well as the ongoing support of my church, family and friends. In particular, I owe a special debt of gratitude to Tony Gadsdon and Lois Poppema, two mighty warriors for the Lord, who painstakingly scoured through the manuscript and made a host of invaluable suggestions. On top of this, I can only marvel at the faithful support in prayer given by Barry Wilson, Isaya Mufiri and so many other truly amazing people.

My hope and prayer is that every reader will be blessed and challenged through encountering this book. It is true that many distinguished authors have expressed themselves on this subject before, often in much more eloquent terms. My fervent hope in tackling the subject afresh, however, is to re-ignite a vibrant debate on a subject which has the potential to impact not only our entire view of scripture and history, but our own place within that template.

Some with a more critical mindset may question my willingness to take the Bible (which, unless indicated otherwise, I have quoted in the New International Version) at its face value, and to accept a traditional view on the authorship of its various books. But its eternal value lies in the fact that we have a supernatural God, unconstrained by the limits of human wisdom and analysis. To him be glory for ever and ever!

# 1 THE WRONG BRIDE?

It is every bride's worst nightmare. It is her wedding night, the day she has looked forward to with mounting anticipation for years, and she discovers that her husband is sleeping with another woman - and not just any other woman, but her own sister! It is difficult to imagine the sense of betrayal, disappointment and rejection. Suddenly, her world has fallen apart.

It might sound like the plot of a contemporary fiction bestseller, but this story of frustrated hopes and shattered dreams is actually thousands of years old. In this ancient tale that originates in chapter 29 of Genesis, Rachel, the bride in question, finds her agonising seven-year wait for marriage cruelly killed off in one fateful night. Suddenly her sister has stolen the prize while she herself now faces a life of ignominy in the shadows, separated from the man she loves.

There is, however, an additional twist to the plot. When morning arrives, Jacob, the bridegroom at the centre of the drama, is equally perturbed. As he comes to his senses, a host of questions floods into his mind. How could it be that he is in bed with Rachel's far less attractive older sister Leah? Can he really have been so drunk the night before? Or was it just too dark to see clearly?

Little by little it begins to dawn upon him that his new father-in-law Laban has double-crossed him and cunningly 'switched' the arrangement at the last minute. But the result is now final. In the culture of the time, having consummated the relationship, it cannot be dissolved, and it is Leah, not his beloved Rachel, who is now Jacob's wife. It is she who, as things stand, will bear his children, carry forward his name, and shape the course of history. Or so the story takes us up to that point.

For many observers across the centuries, something similar has taken place with the Jewish people over the course of time. With their rejection of Jesus as Messiah, God 'switched over' the blessings promised to Israel in the Old Testament to the Gentiles. Whereas in the Old Testament Israel was described as God's 'bride', that role has now been taken over by the church, who will consummate the marriage. She has become the new people of God and there is no longer a purpose for the Jewish people as such - their moment in salvation history has been and gone.

But Rachel and Leah are not alone in their predicament. Intriguingly, the situation of a rejected bride or of two competing female consorts surfaces on a number of other occasions in the Old Testament. In one such story, from earlier in Genesis, Sarah, barren and unable to conceive the child that God has promised to her husband Abraham, offers him her slave-girl Hagar to bring God's plan into being. She has, however, underestimated God's ability to grant her a miracle, and before long *both* her child Isaac and Hagar's son Ishmael are competing for the same inheritance.

Is it possible, once more, to see a parallel here in the relationship between Israel and the church? In his ground-breaking letter to the Galatians, Paul sees the two women as picturing two covenants, one with Israel based on law, and one with the church based on grace:

One covenant is from Mount Sinai and bears children who are to be slaves: this is Hagar. Now Hagar stands for Mount Sinai in Arabia and corresponds to the present city of Jerusalem, because she is in slavery with her children. But the Jerusalem that is above is free, and she is our mother. ... But what does Scripture say? 'Get rid of the slave woman and her son, for the slave woman's son will never share in the inheritance with the free woman's son.' Therefore, brothers and sisters, we are not children of the slave woman, but of the free woman.

(Gal. 4.24-26; 30-31)

But it is not just rivalries between women that attract our attention in Genesis. The men also find their fortunes changing unexpectedly. In one case (Jacob and Esau) the family inheritance is purloined through deception; in another (Reuben) the blessings accorded to the firstborn are forfeited through sin, while in a third (Ephraim and Manasseh); they are 'switched' without warning.

Could these stories also throw light on the relationship between Israel and the church? In chapter 9 of Romans Paul uses the Esau/Jacob conflict to explore this issue once more. In this story Jacob tricks Isaac out of the blessing that in the normal course of events would have gone to Esau. This in turn fulfils God's words to Rebekah about the two twins in her womb, that 'the older will serve the younger' (Gen. 25.23).[1] The same description certainly sums up rather well the troubled tale of relations between Judaism and its ambitious younger brother through history!

While such family strife affects much of the plotline in Genesis, the Rachel story has a much happier ending. Jacob serves his uncle Laban another seven years to win the woman he truly loved in the first place, and *both* she and Leah, despite their continuing rivalry, become the mothers of God's chosen people. Ultimately, they are united and speak together in one voice (Gen. 31.14-16).

But will the future be so rosy for their descendants? Did the Jews finally miss their moment in rejecting Jesus as their Messiah? Or are we again stopping this story halfway before its climax?

In this book I want to challenge the view, prevalent for the last two thousand years and still widespread across many denominations today, that God's promises to Israel have expired and have now been taken over by the church as the 'new Israel'. This teaching, which still dominates in theological seminaries, whether Catholic or Protestant, evangelical or liberal, is sometimes called 'supersessionism' or 'replacement theology'. It is a viewpoint deeply held by many godly people with a passionate love of the scriptures and commitment to the gospel of Jesus Christ.

I am aware that many passages of the Bible, if taken on their own, might appear to support such an understanding of God's purposes throughout history. However, I believe that this view rests on a dangerously selective understanding of scripture and, as we shall see, has resulted in tragic consequences.

What, then, is the alternative? In his letter to the Romans, Paul categorically rejects the view that God has turned his back on the Jewish people forever. Rather, he argues that salvation has come to Gentiles through being 'grafted in' to the olive tree of Israel (11.17) in order to arouse the natural branches, the Jews themselves, to jealousy (v. 11), so that they, too, might accept Jesus as their Messiah. He then describes the 'mystery' that 'Israel has experienced a hardening in part until the full number of the Gentiles has come in, and in this way *all Israel will be saved*' (vv. 25-26).

Let me clear up any confusion that might be caused by the title of this book. I do not believe for a moment that Jesus will return for *two* brides - one being Israel and the other the church. I am using the image of two brides here to reflect the situation as it appears at the present phase of history, to show how God's purposes are often so much larger than our own 'tunnel vision' allows. As I have already pointed out, without *both* Rachel and Leah, Israel could not have existed as a nation in the way we know it today, and would perhaps never have survived the famine that threatened to wipe them out early on (Gen. 42.2). In the same way, I would like to suggest that, without *both* the church *and* Israel, God's purposes will never be complete.

In other words, when Jesus does return it will not be for the church on its own, or Israel on its own, but *both together as a single people of God.* There are several New Testament passages that seem to underline this. For instance, when Jesus talks about '*one* flock and *one* shepherd' he is describing both Jewish sheep and 'other [Gentile] sheep' which are 'not of this sheepfold' (John 10.16). Because he stresses the same idea of complete unity in his statement shortly afterwards that 'I and the Father are *one*' (10.30) it seems natural that when he prays later that we should be *one* as he and the Father are *one* (John 17.22), he has in mind this description of 'us' as Jews and Gentiles together, with himself at the centre.

Similarly, when Paul likens the relationship between a man and his wife to that between Jesus and the church (Eph. 5.31-32) the background is his description of us as 'one new humanity' in Christ composed of Jews *and* Gentiles together (2.15), built on the foundation of the (New Testament) apostles and the (Old Testament) prophets. Without our Jewish adoptive brothers and sisters, we are like the eye saying to the hand, 'I don't need you!' (1 Cor. 12.21).

Our failure to follow this through during the course of history places us in a predicament that would have been unthinkable to many of the writers of the New Testament. Two thousand years on, we are still waiting for Jesus to come back! I do not believe for one moment that he has 'forgotten' his bride. Rather, the bride has *forgotten herself*, and the 'one new humanity' that she represents. Sadly, we still seem as far away as we ever were from approaching that goal.

I could, therefore, equally have called this book 'The Forgetful Bride'. The church has by and large lost sight of a vital part of its calling, and far from embracing its Jewish heritage has turned its back on it. Jews and Christians *need each other* for God's purposes to be complete. As it stands, Judaism and Christianity have both lost their way, and neither are fit in their present state to be the bride that Jesus is returning for.

There are a number of serious implications for Christians which may stem from this. The first is, potentially, a **loss of security.** If the apparently unshakeable promises which God gave to Israel were actually only conditional and temporary in effect, what hope is there for us? If it all depends on our own efforts, what certainty can we have for the future?

Once we begin to dismantle such cast-iron guarantees then all absolutes begin to fall apart. All that we are left with is a sea of meaningless platitudes. The whole continuity and momentum of God's purposes is called into question.

Ultimately we undermine the revealed character of God and simply re-create him in our own image.

Put another way, if God has abandoned Plan 'A' for Plan 'B', what is to stop him tearing up both and opting for Plan 'C' instead? It seems a perfect platform for the claims of Islam, which confidently asserts that it has replaced *both* the Old and New Covenants with something better still.

Thankfully, the Bible does not portray a Creator who constantly shifts the goal-posts. Rather, our destiny depends on the fact that we have a faithful, covenant-keeping God, whose gracious decrees find their ultimate consummation in Jesus himself and his work on the cross. In 2 Corinthians 1.20 Paul assures us that 'no matter how many promises God has made, they are 'Yes' in Christ' (where 'replacement theology' would like to substitute a rather large 'No'!) If our beliefs do not underline this fundamental character and faithfulness of God, we are in deep trouble.

Secondly, we are in danger of creating **a dehumanised Jesus** by plucking him from his true historical background. To conceal his Jewishness risks denying his real humanity and the culture which defined and shaped him, within which he spent his whole life working. Ultimately this blurs the very incarnation itself, suggesting a kind of 'divine superhero' who is somehow not fully human. This is precisely the kind of philosophy John attacks in his first epistle:

Dear friends, do not believe every spirit, but test the spirits to see whether they are from God, because many false prophets have gone out into the world. This is how you can recognise the Spirit of God: *every spirit that acknowledges that Jesus Christ has come in the flesh is from God*, but every spirit that does not acknowledge Jesus is not from God. This is the *spirit of the antichrist*, which you have heard is coming and even now is already in the world.                    (1 John 4.1-3)

We can scarcely ignore the seriousness of this warning. While it may be legitimate to view Jesus through another cultural lens, to see him *only* that way is to impose an alien set of cultural values on him, to preach a different Christ who is ultimately opposed to the genuine one.

We should marvel at the fact that God sovereignly chose the Jewish people to be the vessel through which Jesus would appear on earth as a man, just as he chose Mary to become the final instrument of this plan. Both should be worthy of high respect and honour, on account of this unique calling. Instead, large portions of the church have effectively demonised the one, and deified the other. Both reactions are tragically wide of the mark.

Thirdly, we risk a **loss of Christian identity** by rushing to 'blend in' with the secular world around us, rather than staying close to our roots. We have neglected our rich network of symbols and sacraments whose meaning can only be fully understood against their original Jewish background. In this respect much has become for us like the secular celebration of Christmas, whose *raison d'etre* has become almost completely divorced from the event it actually recalls. So much of the depth of the New

Testament has been lost because we have forgotten its original context.

The result, notes Canon Andrew White, formerly vicar of St. George's Church, Baghdad, is that the church has become largely defenceless against a tide of secularism and liberal humanism which seeks to transform our entire social agenda. He points out that, compared to the robust defence to such winds of change offered by Islam,

much of the Church has become radically disconnected from its core beliefs and principles. Those beliefs and principles are to be found in Judaism and in the Hebrew Bible ... Without them, none of the Church's teachings make any sense nor possesses any authority. Yet much of today's Church displays an indifference to or, worse still, an active hostility towards its Jewish parent that is not only profoundly wrong in itself but is also knocking away the foundations upon which the Church itself stands - and weakening the West in the process.[2]

Where we come from says a lot about who we are. For too long the church has attempted to cut itself off from the life-giving sap of the very olive tree into which God has graciously grafted us (Rom. 11.17). We would do well to consider his advice, originally given to Israel, to 'look to the rock from which you were cut and to the quarry from which you were hewn' (Is. 51.1). Our own foundations rest on the *Jewish* 'apostles and prophets' upon which the Gentiles can become '*fellow* citizens with God's people', who are clearly the Jews themselves (Eph. 2.19-20). Rather than remain in denial about its parentage and family inheritance, the church needs to return home.

A further result of cutting ourselves off from our original moorings is a **devaluing of scripture**. In order to sustain the myth of the church as the replacement for Israel, much of the Old Testament has to be allegorised and 'spiritualised'. The blessings can be applied to the church - but not the curses, which still end up parcelled out to Israel! As Derek White has pointed out, the chapter headings in older versions of the King James Bible illustrate this rather well: Isaiah 49, for example, is entitled 'Restoration of the Church', Isaiah 54 is headed 'The Church is comforted', whereas Isaiah 57 is entitled 'The Jews' idolatry' and Isaiah 59, 'The sins of the Jews'![3] Needless to say, this is a completely skewed approach with no logical basis.

Some go further and abandon the Old Testament altogether. It has served its purpose, but now outlived its value. That once bustling thoroughfare has now been cut off by the ever-advancing motorway of the New Testament into a quiet, lifeless cul-de-sac. This is similar to the approach adopted in the second century AD by Marcion, who jettisoned the entire Old Testament and cut away large portions of the New, removing any references to the God of Israel whom he regarded as a harsh, inferior deity. He was rightly condemned for heresy - yet large sections of the church today seem silently to pay lip-service to some of his assumptions.

Yet when Paul said that '*all* Scripture is God-breathed' (2 Tim. 3.16), it was precisely these *Hebrew* scriptures of the Old Testament to which he was referring. This neither provides sanction for us to ignore it, nor to choose in an arbitrary manner which parts of the old covenant we regard as binding and which are not. It does seem puzzling, for example, for those denominations that do still recognise the continuing validity for Christians of certain Old Testament practices such as tithing, or fasting, or Sabbath observance, to declare God's emphatic promises to Israel as null and void in the same breath. By adopting such a 'pick-and-mix' attitude to the Bible there is a risk of tumbling down a slippery slope where, without realising it, we find ourselves increasingly diluting scripture as the authentic voice of God and pandering instead to human philosophies tailored to the climate of the age we live in.

A further possible consequence may be a **loss of power**. For centuries, many of the charismatic gifts disappeared from the church. In the Old Testament such supernatural gifts were given initially to figures such as Joseph and Moses to bring favour to Jews before *Gentile* rulers. At Pentecost, it was again *Jews* who were given the gifts to witness to *other Jews* who had assembled for a *Jewish* festival from *Gentile* lands. The gifts of the Spirit first came to the Gentiles when a *Jew* was preaching to them.

While no specific conclusions can be attached to these observations, I find it telling that when the church started aligning itself *against* the Jews that the gifts began disappearing. Instead of a Hebrew mindset which saw God actively involved in the mundane details of everyday life, with an openness to the possibility of supernatural intervention in any situation, the church increasingly adopted a mindset drawn from Greek philosophy where God was at one remove from his creation. Within such an outlook it is human logic and reason which are clumsily pressed in to bridge the gap.

If we combine this with a view that God's calling on Israel was conditional (as opposed to Paul's statement in Romans 11.29 that his gifts and call to the Jews are irrevocable), it becomes possible to see the gifts of the Spirit in the same way as a passing phase in God's plan. The idea that the promises to Israel were temporary and were replaced by a 'Plan B' covenant with the church becomes a natural counterpart to the view (sometimes described as 'cessationism') that the gifts of the Spirit were an interim solution, intended all along to be phased out by the completion of the New Testament. While I accept that many Christians sincerely hold to such views, I do not believe that they represent the fulness of God's purposes for the church.

If, instead, we accept that God's purposes are both continuous and cumulative, that Jesus Christ is 'the same yesterday and today and for ever' (Heb. 13.8), our attitude to his grace and provision begins on a much stronger foundation. It may be no coincidence that many of the churches today which are genuinely moving in the signs and wonders supposedly open to all God's people are also churches which understand and revere their Old Testament heritage, which pray for Israel and which see a central continuing role for God's chosen people in the world.

Perhaps the final and most serious consequence of replacement theology, however, has been a **loss of humanity**. Staring through the pages of history, we see one tragic miscarriage of justice after another. The demonising of the Jews that has resulted through the centuries from the church's twisted theological outlook has led to an escalating sequence of discrimination, persecution, banishment and mindless and horrific cruelty. Instead of participating in dismantling the 'dividing wall of hostility' between Jews and Gentiles that Paul tells us Christ came to take away, the church has only reinforced it, to the point that it has created an edifice virtually impenetrable to the gospel. To borrow from another 'two brides' story from the Old Testament, we have been like Peninnah who 'kept provoking' her childless rival Hannah 'in order to irritate her' (1 Sam 1.6), driving Hannah to 'deep anguish' and 'misery' (vv. 10-11).

It is difficult to comprehend why this process continued unchallenged for such a long time. Only with the horrors of Hitler's 'Final Solution' have portions of Christendom begun to wake up from the consequences of the grave and cataclysmic misunderstanding of God's purposes for the Jewish people. But tragically, so many opportunities have been squandered and so many innocent lives thrown away! While the name of Jesus may be music to the ears of the Christian, for the Jew it all too often carries overtones of cruelty and barbarism.

The words of one Jewish writer articulate the reaction that many Jews feel towards the claims of Jesus, given the sheer callousness and mindless brutality of so many of those who have borne his name:

The voice of the blood of millions of our brothers cries out to us from the ground: "No! Christianity is not a religion of love but a religion of unfathomable hate! All history, from ancient times to our own day, is one continuous proof of the total bankruptcy of this religion in all its segments."[4]

It is sad to say that, even today, too many of us within the church still harbour, perhaps quite unconsciously, traces of the theological viewpoint that fuelled much of this rejection in history, an outlook for which even great giants of Christian history such as Origen, Chrysostom and Luther must bear partial responsibility. The irony is that, while both the Magi and Pilate were quick to acknowledge Jesus as 'King of the Jews', we as the church have seemed curiously reluctant to do so! Instead we have preferred 'another Jesus', sanitised for Western culture, producing what I can only describe as 'decaffeinated Christianity'.

I would like, therefore, to suggest that the church has lost its way. Like the prodigal son, she has run away from home, and as with Esau, she has traded her birthright for less than a mess of pottage. With arrogance we have looked down on the Jewish people throughout history, much as the Pharisee looks down on the tax-collector in Jesus' parable, with consequences that have been little short of catastrophic. This is despite Paul's warning to the Romans, in discussing their dependence on their Jewish heritage, that

you do not support the root, but the root supports you. ... Do not be arrogant, but tremble. For if God did not spare the natural branches, he will not spare you either. (Rom. 11.18, 20-21)

In this book I have attempted, however imperfectly, to steer a different course. As we proceed, we will look afresh at God's promises to Israel in the Old Testament and the spiritual battle focused around these. We will then take a further look at those passages often put forward to justify 'replacement theology' to see whether they really say what they are made out to say. Finally, we will try to reassemble the pieces of the theological jigsaw in a somewhat different way, to see what conclusions we can draw, not just for Christianity and Judaism, but also for the challenge posed to both over many centuries by Islam. But first of all, it might be instructive to revisit those sorry pages of church history which show the grim consequences of the assumptions and choices we have made in the past.

# 2 MASSACRE OF THE INNOCENTS

Jesus taught that we should judge a tree by its fruits. What may appear attractive and inviting on the outside can sometimes conceal a bitter taste within. Marxism, for example, looks like a brilliant philosophy on paper, but its consequences, wedded to fallen human nature, have been generally catastrophic. An idea that seems great in a textbook can have very different results in real life.

How does 'replacement theology' fare under the same test? If it is the wonderful news that its advocates claim, we ought to see this reflected in the outcomes it produces. But a brief look at church history in this regard produces a far from encouraging story.

Originally, of course, the church was entirely Jewish in its make-up. It used the Temple for its meetings, the Old

Testament as its scriptures and the Psalms as its hymn-book. Shortly after the death of Jesus it had a membership of several thousand in Jerusalem alone.

As Gentiles began to be admitted in ever-increasing numbers, in response to a vision given to Peter, things became more complicated. Tensions arose over whether Gentile converts needed to be circumcised and to keep the law of Moses. Despite concerted attempts to maintain unity within the body, Jewish and Gentile Christians began more and more to develop an identity separate from each other and to drift apart in their beliefs and practices.

This process became more marked after the fall of Jerusalem in AD 70. The church, increasingly dominated by Gentiles, went through an identity crisis of sorts and began slowly to turn against its Jewish roots. Ignatius, for example, the bishop of Ephesus at the beginning of the second century, declared that:

For if we are still practicing Judaism, we admit that we have not received God's favour ... it is wrong to talk about Jesus Christ and live like Jews. For Christianity did not believe in Judaism, but Judaism in Christianity.[1]

Similarly, the writer of the so-called Epistle of Barnabas, dating from around 130 AD, remarks that:

Take heed to yourselves now, and be not made like unto some, heaping up your sins and saying that the covenant is both theirs and ours. It is ours: but in this way did they finally lose it when Moses had just received it.[2]

He even appears to see the very purpose of Jesus' coming as being to secure the condemnation of the Jewish people:

So then the Son of God came in the flesh for this reason, that he might complete the total of the sins of those who persecuted his prophets to death.[3]

Justin Martyr, in the middle of the century, begins turning up the heat. In his *Dialogue with Trypho* he comments on the recent Roman destruction of Jerusalem in 135 AD, and the scattering of the Jewish people which resulted:

The custom of circumcising the flesh, handed down from Abraham, was given to you as a distinguishing mark, to set you off from other nations and from us Christians. The purpose of this was that you and only you might suffer the afflictions that are now justly yours; that only your land be desolated, and your cities ruined by fire, that the fruits of your land be eaten by strangers before your very eyes; that not one of you be permitted to enter your city of Jerusalem.[4]

Justin set the pattern for many later Christian writers. In the third century Origen declared that:

We may thus assert in utter confidence that the Jews will not return to their earlier situation, for they have committed the most abominable of crimes, in forming this conspiracy against the Saviour of the human race … hence the city where Jesus suffered was necessarily destroyed, the Jewish nation was driven from its country, and another people was called by God to the blessed election.[5]

By the fourth century there are signs of such attitudes beginning to harden within the growing Christian community. In AD 306, for example, the Synod of Elvira in Spain forbade marriages, sexual relationships and friendships of any kind between Christians and Jews, and later in the century a similar ruling became enforced across the entire Roman Empire.

With the Council of Nicaea in AD 325 the decision was made to separate the celebration of Easter from the Jewish Passover, and Christians were forbidden to celebrate Passover with Jews, or to engage in formal worship on the Jewish Sabbath. The newly-converted Emperor Constantine, ratifying the decree, is quoted as saying: 'Let us then have nothing in common with the detestable Jewish crowd. ... and withdraw ourselves from all participation in their baseness.'[6]

In AD 329, with Christianity now having switched from a persecuted religion to having the full backing of the state, conversion to Judaism could result in punitive sanctions. A further edict in 353 allowed for a convert's property to be confiscated and taken over by the state. By 409, a Jew attempting to convert a Christian could be held guilty of High Treason.

In the year 388 a Christian mob led by the local bishop burned down the synagogue of Callinicum in Mesopotamia. The Emperor Theodosius ordered that the local bishop compensate the Jews by having the church subsidise the reconstruction of a new synagogue, but he was forced by Bishop Ambrose of Milan to back down or have the church's sacraments withdrawn from him.

Around this time we see a bitter war of invective being waged in some Christian circles without restriction.

Ambrose (c. 340-397), to whom we have already referred, wrote:

a synagogue [is] a home of unbelief, a house of impiety, a receptacle of folly, which God himself has condemned. [7]

John Chrysostom (344-407 AD) was also strident in his condemnation. In the first of *Eight Orations against Judaizing Christians* (387-388) he wrote as follows:

But the synagogue is not only a brothel and a theatre; it also is a den of robbers and a lodging for wild beasts ... It is not merely a lodging place for robbers and cheats but also for demons. Here the slayers of Christ gather together, here the cross is driven out, here God is blasphemed, here the Father is ignored, here the Son is outraged, here the grace of the Spirit is rejected. Does not greater harm come from this place since the Jews themselves are demons? ... and so we must hate both them and their synagogue all the more.[8]

Chrysostom's attacks, however, were not only made against synagogue worship, but were also directed at a more personal level:

The Jews ... live for their bellies, they gape for the things of this world, their condition is not better than that of pigs or goats because of their wanton ways and excessive gluttony. ... Must you share a greeting with them and exchange a bare word? Must you not turn away from them since they are the common disgrace and infection of the whole world? Have they not come to every form of wickedness? ... they became more savage than any wild beast.[9]

Strongly-worded though such comments are, they seem almost mild when we compare what we find in the writings of Ephrem the Syrian (306-373). This excerpt from one of his poems makes very stark reading today:

I hate the Jewish dead!
I loathe their bones in Sheol.
If only there was a way I could get rid of their bones
from Sheol, for they make the place stink!
By the Holy Spirit, I'm astonished at how long I've dwelt
among a People who smell as rank as their way of life![10]

Within this climate, under the influence of the church, restrictions against the Jews started becoming enshrined in imperial law. In 438 all Jews were excluded from public service and forbidden to build new places of worship. In 553 Justinian forbade the reading of the Mishnah and restricted what could be taught in synagogues. He also attempted to close down all synagogues in North Africa, and converted some into churches. In 614 Emperor Heraclius outlawed Judaism completely in the Byzantine Empire and many Jews were compelled to convert.

With the Jews in Europe already feeling the heat of such sporadic attacks, they could draw little comfort from the flood of oppressive restrictions brought in by local church councils and synods that followed during this time and in successive centuries. In AD 538, the Third Council of Orleans forbade Jews from appearing in public in the latter half of holy week (in later centuries, this became a necessity, as Jews were liable to be stoned or whipped by unruly Christian mobs at this time). In 653 the Eighth Council of Toledo banned circumcision and required Jewish converts to Christianity to stone or burn to death those of their number who relapsed. The following year the

Visigothic rulers in Spain, aided and abetted by the church, made it illegal for Jews to observe Passover or other Feasts, keep the Sabbath or observe Jewish dietary laws.

This spate of harsh and oppressive rulings culminated in 694 with the Fourteenth Council of Toledo which required all Jews to be sold into slavery, with their property confiscated, and all Jewish children over the age of seven to be forcibly removed and educated in monasteries. Such measures provided a frightening foretaste of the storm of persecution that was to be unleashed on the Iberian peninsula almost eight centuries later.

Against the background of these repeated waves of persecution, it is a miracle that the Jews survived at all. Some estimates suggest that, in the first nine centuries of the church, the entire population of Jews in the world was reduced to just an eighth of those who had lived in the time of Jesus.[11] Although, within the church, there were a few dissenting voices against this tide of cruelty and ill-treatment, the general outlook was bleak.

While such systematic persecution was sporadic and often short-lived, conditions began to worsen again for many Jews in the Middle Ages. In 1050, the Synod of Narbonne prohibited Christians from living in Jewish homes. The Synod of Gerona in 1078 imposed a requirement on Jews to pay taxes to the Church. The Third Lateran Council of 1179 severely restricted medical care that could be provided by Christians to Jews and restricted Jews to living in certain designated areas.

With the Fourth Lateran Council of 1215 these restrictions were extended: Jews were excluded from holding any public office and were required to wear special clothing to distinguish them from Christians, a ruling reinforced by the Synod of Narbonne of 1227 which required them to wear an oval badge. The Council of Beziers in 1246 threatened withdrawal of the sacraments and Christian burial rites to anyone being treated by a Jewish doctor. The Council of Basel (1431-1443) excluded them from attending universities, forbade them from studying the Talmud, and forced them to attend Christian sermons.

For Jews wishing to embrace Christianity, blood-curdling oaths were initiated, such as this one, sometimes wrongly attributed to Constantine, but dating from the Middle Ages:

I renounce all customs, rites, legalisms, unleavened breads and sacrifices of lambs of the Hebrews, and all the other feasts of the Hebrews, sacrifices, prayers, aspirations, purifications, sanctifications, and propitiations, and fasts and new moons, and Sabbaths, and superstitions, and hymns and chants, and observances and synagogues and the food and drink of the Hebrews; in one word, I renounce absolutely everything Jewish, every Law, rite and custom … and if afterwards I shall wish to deny and return to Jewish superstition, or shall be found eating with Jews, or feasting with them, or secretly conversing and condemning the Christian religion instead of openly confuting them and condemning their vain faith, then let the trembling of Cain and the leprosy of Gehazi cleave to me, as well as the legal punishments to which I acknowledge myself liable. And may I be an anathema in the world to come, and may my soul be set down with Satan and the devils.[12]

In law-courts, other appalling oaths were forced on Jews who gave testimony. Many such oaths persisted for centuries - in Romania, as recently as 1912! One such oath, in use in Frankfurt at the end of the fourteenth century, compelled Jews to repeat the words:

And may that sulphur and pitch flow down upon your neck that flowed over Sodom and Gomorrah, and the same pitch that flowed over Babylon flow over you, but two hundred times more, and may the earth envelop and swallow you up as it did Dathan and Abiram. And may your dust never join other dust, and your earth never join other earth in the bosom of Master Abraham if what you say is not true and right.[13]

Against this background we see a whole range of sporadic but repeated attacks such as forced conversions, the kidnapping of children for baptism, the destruction of synagogues, cramming large numbers into overcrowded ghettos, and repeated massacres. The Crusades in particular brought appalling atrocities: in the First Crusade alone thousands of Jews were butchered, many others forcibly baptised, even before the Crusaders had reached the Holy Land itself. Of the attack in the German town of Worms in May 1096 Rabbi Eliezer bar Nathan recorded that

the enemies and oppressors set upon the Jews who were in their homes, pillaging, and murdering men, women, and children, young and old. They destroyed the houses and pulled down the stairways, looting and plundering; and they took the holy Torah, trampled it in the mud of the streets, and tore it and desecrated it amidst ridicule and laughter.[14]

Later that same month the Crusaders reached Mainz. A contemporary chronicler, Raymond of Aachen, the chaplain to the leader of the Provençal army, described how they treated those Jews who had taken sanctuary:

Breaking the bolts and doors, they killed the Jews, about seven hundred in number, who in vain resisted the force and attack of so many thousands. They killed the women, also, and with their swords pierced tender children of whatever age and sex. The Jews, seeing that their Christian enemies were attacking them and their children, and that they were sparing no age, likewise fell upon one another, brother, children, wives, and sisters, and thus they perished at each other's hands. Horrible to say, mothers cut the throats of nursing children with knives and stabbed others, preferring them to perish thus by their own hands rather than to be killed by the weapons of the uncircumcised.[15]

When the Crusaders finally got to Jerusalem they accelerated this frenzy of killing, almost in the spirit of a Christian *jihad*. Commenting with apparent approval on the indiscriminate slaughter of Muslims and Jews in the Crusaders' attack on Jerusalem, the same writer noted that:

Wonderful sights were to be seen. ... Piles of heads, hands, and feet were to be seen in the streets of the city. It was necessary to pick one's way over the bodies of men and horses. But these were small matters compared to what happened at the Temple of Solomon ... men rode in blood up to their knees and bridle reins. Indeed, it was a just and splendid judgment of God that this place should be filled with the blood of the unbelievers, since it had suffered so long from their blasphemies. The city was filled with corpses and blood.[16]

Almost a thousand Jews took refuge in the synagogue. Emboldened by their success in battle, the Crusaders set it on fire before marching around, singing, 'Christ, we adore thee.' Everyone inside, men, women and children, lost their lives in the inferno.

Although many Medieval Popes sought to protect the Jews (amazingly, one Pope, Anacletus II, was himself of Hebrew descent), some were far less enlightened. In 1205 Pope Innocent III wrote to the archbishops of Sens and Paris that 'the Jews, by their own guilt, are consigned to perpetual servitude because they crucified the Lord ... As slaves rejected by God, in whose death they wickedly conspire, they shall by the effect of this very action, recognise themselves as the slaves of those whom Christ's death set free ... '[17]. In 1240 Gregory IX ordered the confiscation of Jewish literature and two years later 24 wagon-loads of books were ordered to be burnt in public: thereafter book-burning became a common practice.

In the mid-thirteenth the so-called 'Blood Libel' began circulating in England that Jews murdered Christian children in the preparation of their Passover matzos. This belief was extraordinary given that the Old Testament forbids the consumption of blood of any kind and shows an amazing degree of gullibility. Many random acts of atrocity took place as a result, and the rumour began to circulate widely across Europe. In 1279 all Jews in London were arrested (on a different matter) and in 1290 they were expelled from England and their possessions seized by the crown. It was not until an edict of Oliver Cromwell in 1656 that they were permitted to return.

Other countries organised similar forced expulsions: In France the entire Jewish population was arrested on a single day in 1306 and forced to leave the country; after a further expulsion in 1394 they were unable to return until the French Revolution in 1789.

At the end of the following century Spain and later Portugal followed suit. The background to these forced migrations was particularly tragic: Spain had been host to one of the largest Jewish communities in Europe. However, after the marriage of Ferdinand and Isabella in 1469, many Jews who had been pressured to convert under previous rulers were suspected to be secretly practising Judaism. Those who confessed 'voluntarily' were imprisoned for life and had all their possessions confiscated; the remainder were tortured by the Spanish Inquisition until the required confession was forced out, and then burnt to death. After fourteen years in which thousands were subjected to such torture and death by burning, an edict was issued in 1492 giving Spanish Jews the choice of exile or compulsory baptism. Almost all Jews took the opportunity to leave at this time.

In the German-speaking world the Jews fared little better; many were accused of causing the Black Death by poisoning wells. Under torture, false confessions were extracted which were then used as a pretext for destroying entire Jewish communities. In several cases, such as in Strasbourg and Basel in 1349, hundreds of innocent people were herded into wooden buildings which were then set on fire.

Even the New World could not escape the tide of persecution. In 1596, Luis de Carvajal, the former governor of the province of Nuevo León in Mexico, aroused the jealousy of the Viceroy, who exposed the fact that he was secretly observing Jewish practices. As a result many of his family were implicated. His nephew of the same name, sentenced to death at just thirty years old, was subjected to torture so brutal that he revealed the names of over a 120 of his fellow Jews. Afterwards he was forced to listen as the 'heretics' he exposed, including his own mother and two of his sisters, were tortured in an adjoining cell. The following day they were burned alive.

With all these events taking place across the Catholic world, many with the tacit or quite open support of the church, one might have hoped for better with the breath of fresh air brought in by the Protestant reformation. Sadly, this is far from the case. While Luther may have started out with a more favourable view of the Jews, what he wrote in 1543, described by one recent commentator as 'the first work of modern antisemitism'[18] is sadly one of the harshest attacks on Judaism ever penned:

What shall we Christians do with this rejected and condemned people, the Jews? Since they live among us, we dare not tolerate their conduct, now that we are aware of their lying and reviling and blaspheming. If we do, we become sharers in their lies, cursing and blasphemy ... I shall give you my sincere advice:

First to set fire to their synagogues or schools and to bury and cover with dirt whatever will not burn, so that no man will ever again see a stone or cinder of them. This is to be done in honour of our Lord and of Christendom, so that God might see that we are Christians ...

Second, I advise that their houses also be razed and destroyed. ...

Third, I advise that all their prayer books and Talmudic writings, in which such idolatry, lies, cursing and blasphemy are taught, be taken from them.

Fourth, I advise that their rabbis be forbidden to teach henceforth on pain of loss of life and limb. ...

Fifth, I advise that safe-conduct on the highways be abolished completely for the Jews. ... For you, too, must not and cannot protect them unless you wish to become participants in their abominations in the sight of God.

Sixth, I advise that usury be prohibited to them, and that all cash and treasure of silver and gold be taken from them and put aside for safekeeping. ...

How does it happen that we poor Christians nourish and enrich such an idle and lazy people, such a useless, evil pernicious people, such blasphemous enemies of God, receiving nothing in return but their curses and defamation and every misfortune they may inflict on us or wish us? ...

Christ ... declares that they are venomous, bitter, vindictive, tricky serpents, assassins, and children of the devil who sting and work harm stealthily wherever they cannot do it openly. ... next to the devil, a Christian has no more bitter and galling foe than a Jew. There is no other to whom we accord as many benefactions and from whom we suffer as much as we do from these base children of the devil, this brood of vipers.[19]

Calvin, though sometimes more generous in his comments, could also express himself in similar terms:

Their rotten and unbending stiffneckedness deserves that they be oppressed unendingly and without measure or end and that they die in their misery without the pity of anyone.[20]

In those areas of Europe under Orthodoxy, meanwhile, things fared no better. Between 1648 and 1649, about three hundred Jewish communities were destroyed in Ukraine, and around 100,000 lost their lives. Today, the instigator,

Bogdan Chmielnicki (1593-1657), is still revered in Ukraine as a national hero and his portrait features on banknotes. With the frequent connivance of the Orthodox Church, anti-Jewish pogroms became commonplace, particularly in Russia in the early twentieth century, and thousands of Jews were mercilessly slaughtered. In the Kishinev pogrom, which began on Easter Sunday 1903 in the capital of what is now Moldova, 47 Jews were killed, 700 houses were destroyed, and 600 stores looted. The New York Times later reported as follows:

The mob was led by priests, and the general cry, "Kill the Jews," was taken up all over the city. The Jews were taken wholly unaware and were slaughtered like sheep. The dead number 120 and the injured about 500. The scenes of horror attending this massacre are beyond description. Babes were literally torn to pieces by the frenzied and bloodthirsty mob. The local police made no attempt to check the reign of terror. At sunset the streets were piled with corpses and wounded. Those who could make their escape fled in terror, and the city is now practically deserted of Jews.[21]

And so the story continues, outrage after outrage, tragedy after tragedy. We, of course, know the end of the story, and how it reaches its inexorable climax in the ovens of Auschwitz and Treblinka. Under German Chancellor Adolf Hitler, cold-blooded murder became automated with almost machine-like precision. Yet many of the Nazis' most fervent supporters were ardent churchgoers. Hypnotised by a century of deadening liberal theology, the majority of the German church walked the aisle with them to the very precipice of hell itself.

The Nazis used Luther's writings and indeed the whole gamut of Christian history to justify their atrocities. In a meeting with Roman Catholic Bishop Wilhelm Berning of Osnabrück on April 26, 1933, Hitler declared:

I have been attacked because of my handling of the Jewish question. The Catholic Church considered the Jews pestilent for fifteen hundred years, put them in ghettos, etc., because it recognized the Jews for what they were. In the epoch of liberalism the danger was no longer recognized. I am moving back toward the time in which a fifteen-hundred-year-long tradition was implemented.[22]

It is probably no exaggeration to say that virtually every horror perpetrated by the Nazis has its roots in some decision or statement made by the church at some stage in its history. The only difference is that Hitler carried out the barbarity on an industrial scale. The Holocaust provides six million reasons why the church has got it wrong.

Raul Hillberg, writing about this inexorable historical progression, comments as follows:

Since the fourth century after Christ there have been three anti-Jewish policies: [forced] conversion, expulsion, and annihilation. The second appeared as an alternative to the first, and the first emerged as an alternative to the second ... The missionaries of Christianity had said in effect: You have no right to live among us as Jews. The secular rulers who followed proclaimed: You have no right to live among us. The Nazis at last decreed: You have no right to live.[23]

For Christians, the catastrophe of the 'Final Solution' is something we simply cannot afford to forget. Commenting on the 'unspeakable cruelty' of Auschwitz as a 'new and terrifying stage in history', Kenneth Cracknell suggests that

Christians need to ponder whether the Holocaust merely serves as an eternal warning or whether it is the first station on the road to the extermination of all peoples and the suicide of humanity.[24]

How then, should we respond today? Will we simply wash our hands of the past or airbrush these events from our history? Or will we face up to the grim spectre of our past a re-examine our hearts and our beliefs? Like that of Abel, our brother's blood still cries out from the ground. As Rabbi Irving Greenberg once said, 'No statement, theological or otherwise, should be made that would not be credible in the presence of burning children.'[25]

Clearly, the church still has much soul-searching to do to truly address these issues. How could we have gone so far off-course? Where, in this appalling sequence of events, is there any trace of the gospel of love, peace and reconciliation that Jesus preached? Is 'replacement theology' a valid response to scripture, or simply anti-Semitism arrayed in polite evening dress? Could it be, behind a smiling countenance, that a hideous theological monstrosity is lurking?

In Chapter Four we will begin to explore some of these issues, and the spiritual dynamic that might lie behind them. But first, we need to blow the cobwebs away and take a good, hard look at the Old Testament. What really were God's purposes for Israel as a nation?

# 3 UNBREAKABLE PROMISES

Anyone who contemplates the wonders of the natural world around us may sense a reflection of a vital supernatural principle. God 'grows' his kingdom from small, apparently insignificant things, which gather momentum and fruitfulness as they unfold. Jesus explains this clearly in two parables in Mark's Gospel:

He also said, 'This is what the kingdom of God is like. A man scatters seed on the ground. Night and day, whether he sleeps or gets up, the seed sprouts and grows, though he does not know how. All by itself the soil produces corn – first the stalk, then the ear, then the full grain in the ear. As soon as the corn is ripe, he puts the sickle to it, because the harvest has come.'

Again he said, 'What shall we say the kingdom of God is like, or what parable shall we use to describe it? It is like a mustard seed, which is the smallest of all seeds on earth. Yet when planted, it grows and becomes the largest of all garden plants, with such big branches that the birds can perch in its shade.' (Mark 4.26-32)

As Jesus reminds us here, seeds are extraordinary things. They have the ability to remain dormant and apparently lifeless for long periods. Yet within them resides the principle of infinite life, and given the right conditions they will spring into action. Outwardly there may be little sign of change, but quietly, slowly, invisibly, behind the scenes, a remarkable transformation takes place. Inside a single acorn lies not just the blueprint for an oak tree, but an irreversible formula for countless forests of trees that could potentially engulf an entire continent.

In the Bible, a person or thing completely surrendered to the purposes of God can also take on these life-like principles of multiplication. For example, in the gospels, when a boy surrenders his packed lunch it becomes, in the hands of Christ, a banquet for a multitude. Jesus uses this as a picture to describe the giving of his own body, to be sacrificed on the cross for many (John 6.48-51). He later says that 'unless a grain of wheat falls to the ground and dies, it remains only a single seed. But if it dies, it produces many seeds' (John 12.24).

Jumping back two thousand years, we can see the same pattern of sacrifice and fruitfulness in the story of Abraham. When he surrenders to God his most precious possession, his beloved son Isaac, God makes him an extraordinary promise:

'I swear by myself, declares the LORD, that because you have done this and have not withheld your son, your only son, I will surely bless you and make your descendants *as numerous as the stars in the sky and as the sand on the seashore*. Your descendants will take possession of the cities of their enemies, and through your offspring all nations on earth will be blessed, because you have obeyed me.' (Gen. 22.16-18).

The Hebrew word for 'descendants' here is 'seed'. God is planning to multiply Abraham beyond his wildest dreams, in a manner that would impact the whole world. If Abraham were to have looked into a pool of water, he would have seen his own reflection. When God looked at him, he saw an entire nation!

It is worth considering the remarkable implications of the language that God uses to confirm this, as the scope of it would have been completely beyond Abraham's grasp: 'I will surely bless you and make your descendants *as numerous as the stars in the sky and as the sand on the seashore*' (v. 17).

How would Abraham have understood this? The number of stars visible to him on a really clear night would at best have been a few thousand. In fact, the greatest astronomer of the ancient world, Hipparchus, listed just 850 stars in his catalogue. This was expanded by Ptolemy of Alexandria in the second century AD to 1,022.

By contrast, the number of grains of sand in all the beaches in the world is mind-boggling - the Australian scientist Chris Flynn has suggested as a very crude estimate $10^{24}$ - that is, a ten with twenty-four zeros after it![1] How do we solve this apparent disparity, then, between a mere scattering of stars and an almost endless quantity of sand?

Here modern astronomy comes to the rescue. The universe as we now know it is indescribably more vast than anything that could have been known in Abraham's day. The remarkable thing is that Flynn's calculation for the number of grains of sand on the earth's beaches actually matches with dazzling agreement a recent estimate for the number of stars in the universe given by the European Space Agency![2]

What is staggering here is not just the accuracy of the Bible thousands of years before the advent of the telescope, but the extravagance of the promise being made to a single individual. It makes God's later declaration in Isaiah seem like a colossal understatement:

'When I called him he was only one man,
  and *I blessed him and made him many.*' (Is. 51.2)

But this extraordinary promise was not actually dependent on Abraham's own actions in offering up Isaac. God was simply underlining what he had already guaranteed to Abraham previously, when having a son was still a biological impossibility (Gen. 15.4-5). The Bible declares that he 'believed the LORD, and he credited it to him as righteousness' (v. 6). Yet the promise is given to Abraham, not just of offspring, but of land, *even before this response of faith* (12.7).

Moreover, this is underpinned by a solemn covenant with Abraham in which, according to the custom of the times, several sacrificial animals are killed and split in half. As I pointed out in an earlier book, *But is he God?*, it was normal at this period for both parties to an agreement to walk between the broken animal carcasses to show visually the dire consequences that would fall on either side should the terms of the covenant be broken.[3] Yet, with great significance for the future course of events, it is only God himself, in the form of a smoking brazier and a blazing torch, who does this, suggesting that *he alone* would bear the punishment should Abraham's descendants break the terms of the covenant.

In other words, the covenant given to Abraham was *unconditional*, made regardless of how Abraham would respond, with its terms underwritten by God himself. Moreover it was made not just with Abraham but also with his offspring (literally, 'seed'), with whom it would be an *everlasting* covenant, with the land offered as an *everlasting* possession (17.7-8).

And so, over the course of time, the seed put roots down, bore shoots and flourished. From Abraham's tiny mustard-seed of faith, a nation emerged. Their calling was to be unique: they were to be God's 'treasured possession', a 'kingdom of priests and a holy nation' (Ex. 19.5-6), 'chosen of all the families of the earth' (Amos 3.2), distinct and set apart from every other people (Num. 23.9; Esther 3.8) to witness to God's uniqueness and his saving power (Is. 43.10-12).

It was not, of course, an entirely smooth process: repeatedly they were unfaithful to God, disobeying him and reaping dire consequences as a result. Yet despite this, the risk of total abandonment by God was always forestalled by the unconditional nature of the covenant he had made with Abraham. We can see this, for instance, in Deuteronomy 9.27, where Moses appeals to the unbreakable guarantees God has given in the past:

'Remember your servants Abraham, Isaac and Jacob. Overlook the stubbornness of this people, their wickedness and their sin.'

Furthermore, even when, in Leviticus and Deuteronomy, the consequences of rebellion are spelt out in gut-wrenching detail, the everlasting and unconditional nature of God's covenant with Israel remains intact:

'Yet in spite of this, when they are in the land of their enemies, I will not reject them or abhor them so as to destroy them completely, breaking my covenant with them. I am the LORD their God. But for their sake I will remember the covenant with their ancestors whom I brought out of Egypt in the sight of the nations to be their God. I am the LORD.'
(Lev. 26.44-45)

Psalm 94 also affirms the unchanging nature of God's purposes for Israel, despite impending judgement on the nations around:

For the LORD will not reject his people;
    he will never forsake his inheritance. (v. 14)

Moreover, God had, and still has, a plan to rescue Israel from its constant cycle of backsliding. In Ezekiel 36, he declares:

'For I will take you out of the nations; I will gather you from all the countries and bring you back into your own land. I will sprinkle clean water on you, and you will be clean; I will cleanse

you from all your impurities and from all your idols. I will give
you a new heart and put a new spirit in you; I will remove from
you your heart of stone and give you a heart of flesh. And I will
put my Spirit in you and move you to follow my decrees and be
careful to keep my laws. Then you will live in the land I gave
your ancestors; you will be my people, and I will be your God.'

(Ezek. 36.24-28)

Notice here that this promise is again initiated *entirely by
God himself*, and that the blessings follow *after* the Jews
return to their own land.

The same promise appears in Jeremiah 31, which describes
a *new* covenant that God will make *specifically with Israel
and Judah* (v. 31) where he promises that

'I will put my law in their minds and write it on their hearts. I
will be their God, and they will be my people.' (31.33)

There then follows one of the remarkable declarations ever
given in scripture:

Thus says the LORD,
who gives the sun for light by day
    and the fixed order of the moon and the stars for light by
night,
who stirs up the sea so that its waves roar—
    the LORD of hosts is his name:
'*If this fixed order departs
    from before me, declares the LORD,
then shall the offspring of Israel cease
    from being a nation before me for ever.*'
Thus says the LORD:
'If the heavens above can be measured,
    and the foundations of the earth below can be explored,
then I will cast off all the offspring of Israel

for all that they have done,
declares the LORD.'                                        (Jer. 31.35-37 ESV)

In other words, the promises to Israel are tied to the very laws which govern the universe. To break them would be like overturning the very law of gravity itself![4]

The crowning climax of the plan, of course, was the coming of the anointed servant, the Messiah, who would *be* the people's righteousness (Jer. 23.6), who would *himself* be the covenant between God and his people (Is. 42.6) and who through rejection and death would bring peace, healing and restoration to Israel (Is. 53.1-6) by bearing their iniquities (53.11).

But God's purposes were not restricted to Israel alone. Throughout the Old Testament, there are hints that, though focusing on the Jewish people, God's plans to restore his kingdom on earth would ultimately have a much wider scope. When God first reveals himself to Abraham, he declares:

'I will bless those who bless you,
 and whoever curses you I will curse;
and all peoples on earth
 will be blessed through you.' (Gen. 12.3)

This promise is then repeated to Isaac (26.4) and to Jacob (28.14). Israel is called to be a silent witness to the nations around (Deut. 4.6-8) and ultimately, a bearer of salvation to the Gentiles (Jonah 3.1-10).

46

Throughout the Old Testament, the boundaries of Israel are never set in stone. It is a 'mixed multitude' who left Egypt with the Jewish nation. In Numbers 10.29-32, Moses invites a Midianite, his wife's brother, to remain with them and share in the blessings of the people. In the book of Ruth we find a Gentile girl cleaving to her Jewish mother-in-law and as a result becoming an ancestor of King David.

Such outsiders are to be accorded equal treatment. Joseph's children Ephraim and Manasseh are born of a Gentile wife and yet receive a full inheritance in Israel. Leviticus 19.34 declares that 'You shall treat the stranger who sojourns with you as the native among you, and you shall love him as yourself' (ESV). In Ezekiel 47.22 the 'foreigners residing among you' are to be treated as 'native-born Israelites'.

But the vision in the prophets, and in particular Isaiah, becomes much bigger than simply drawing in isolated individuals. In Isaiah 55 Israel is told that

'you will summon nations you know not,
 and nations you do not know will come running to you,
because of the LORD your God,
 the Holy One of Israel,
 for he has endowed you with splendour.' (v. 5)

In Isaiah 60 the same image appears:

'See, darkness covers the earth
 and thick darkness is over the peoples,
but the LORD rises upon you
 and his glory appears over you.
Nations will come to your light,
 and kings to the brightness of your dawn.' (vv. 2-3)

The ultimate goal seems to be expressed in Malachi 1.11:

'My name will be great among the nations, from where the sun rises to where it sets. In every place incense and pure offerings will be brought to me, because my name will be great among the nations,' says the LORD Almighty.

Once more these promises become particularly focused in the coming of the Messiah, who would reign on David's throne, and who would bring righteous government, peace and justice to the whole earth. He will 'stand as a banner for the peoples' and 'the nations will rally to him' (Is. 11.10). After the description of his death for sinners in Isaiah 53, references to a Gentile ingathering become more detailed and more frequent.

Yet Messiah's task here is clearly an expansion of that assignment given to Israel herself. In Isaiah this is expressed through an intriguing overlap of meaning. On the one hand, the 'servant' who achieves these things is none other than the nation of Israel herself:

He said to me, '*You are my servant,*
  *Israel,* in whom I will display my splendour.' (49.3)

On the other, the servant also appears to be someone *within* Israel:

'It is too small a thing for you to be my servant
  to restore the tribes of Jacob
  and bring back those of Israel I have kept.
I will also make you a light for the Gentiles,
  that my salvation may reach to the ends of the earth.' (49. 6)

Here then, is the key: the blessing to the nations that comes through discovering the Jewish Messiah is *entirely dependent* on God's unbreakable covenant with Israel itself. At no point in the Old Testament is there any clear indication that in achieving this God will somehow *exchange* his favour from Israel to the Gentile nations, or disinherit her from the promises he made to Abraham.

Indeed, we have to ask whether, in God's economy, such an uprooting or a 'switch' of blessing could be really be possible. Numbers 36.9, for example, specifically forbids the transfer of inheritance from one tribe to another. Why should God allow this on a wider scale? Given the nature of the unbreakable assurances he gave to Israel, any attempt to do so would call his entire character and faithfulness into question.

In short, it is difficult to find anywhere in the Old Testament that would provide firm grounds for teaching 'replacement theology'. God's promises to Abraham, Isaac and Jacob are permanent, independent of response and therefore could only come to others through an *enlargement*, rather than a *replacement*, of the original guarantee. And in references to a *new* covenant in Isaiah, Jeremiah and Ezekiel, the promises continue to be centred upon Israel herself.

But what of the New Testament? Some would cite Hebrews 8.13 to demonstrate that Israel's special calling is no longer valid:

By calling this covenant 'new', he has made the first one obsolete; and what is obsolete and outdated will soon disappear.

It is easy to forget, however, that this is a passage written *by a Jew* to believers who were *Jews* comparing two *Jewish* covenants, the Mosaic, based in law, and the New, centred on grace, specifically made (as we pointed out earlier) with the house of Israel and Judah. 'Soon' is a very elastic word from God's timescale (Rev. 22.20)! Moreover, the very passage from Jeremiah that it quotes goes on to state, as we saw earlier, that God's promises to Israel are as fixed and unalterable as the very laws which govern the universe itself.

Even in the New Testament, therefore, these solemn assurances made to Israel remain the possession of the Jewish people despite their continuing state of unbelief. Thus Paul can write as follows:

Theirs is the adoption to sonship; theirs the divine glory, the covenants, the receiving of the law, the temple worship and the promises.                                     (Rom. 9.4).

Later he emphasises that because of these covenants made with the patriarchs, God's love for Israel remains unchanged and that his 'gifts and his call are irrevocable' (11.28-29). It is through God's sovereign act of grace that the Gentiles can now also be included within these promises (11.17-21).

All this seems to express rather neatly the parable of the mustard seed that we read at the beginning of the chapter. Abraham's tiny mustard seed of faith has grown to become a mighty tree, in which all the 'birds of the air' find shade. The Gentiles find a place not by uprooting the tree, but lodging within its branches.

Elsewhere in the New Testament the same point is underlined. As they bless Israel, the Gentiles receive blessing themselves. Jesus, for example, is willing to countenance visiting the house of a Gentile centurion, an act normally unthinkable for an observant Jew, because local Jewish elders have insisted that 'he loves our nation and has built our synagogue' (Luke 7.4-5). Likewise another centurion, Cornelius, is the first Gentile to experience an outpouring of the Spirit on his household because 'he gave generously to help the Jewish people, and was regular in his prayers to God' (Acts 10.2).

But if this is the case, how could his later successors have got it so wrong? How could it be that such great, anointed men of God as Chrysostom or Luther could stoop to such callous, ill-tempered verbal assaults on the very people through whom their own salvation had been secured? How could the church through the centuries have strayed so far in spirit from the very Jewish Messiah who founded it? And how could a modern, civilised nation such as Germany in the 1930s descend to the unspeakable brutality of the Third Reich, with the full support of two-thirds of the German church? Is there a common factor behind these things? These are questions that we will begin to explore in the next chapter.

# 4 THE SPOILER

Given the firm, unbreakable assurances that God gave to the descendants of Abraham, Isaac and Jacob in the Old Testament, several inevitable questions arise: *Why* did the church fall to such depths of barbarity and hatred towards the very race to which Jesus belonged? And where was God in all of this? Why would he allow his chosen people to experience all the sufferings and humiliations of the last two thousand years? Could he not have intervened, for example, to stop the Holocaust? Could the very nature of the trials that the Jews have endured suggest that, at least for a time, they have forfeited his blessing? Was it all a punishment for rejecting their Messiah?

Certainly, from a New Testament perspective, the Jewish rejection of Jesus was a mistake of catastrophic proportions. It is clearly possible to see the events of the next two thousand years as the inevitable consequence of this. Without doubt, the fearful list of warnings in Deuteronomy and in later prophetic books bears an uncanny resemblance to many of the woes the Jews have suffered in the last twenty centuries, culminating in the savage cruelty of Nazi Germany:

You will become a thing of horror, a byword and an object of ridicule among all the peoples where the LORD will drive you.
(Deut. 28.37)

The LORD will bring a nation against you from far away, from the ends of the earth, like an eagle swooping down, a nation whose language you will not understand, a fierce-looking nation without respect for the old or pity for the young.
(Deut. 28.49-50)

Among those nations you will find no repose, no resting place for the sole of your foot. There the LORD will give you an anxious mind, eyes weary with longing, and a despairing heart. You will live in constant suspense, filled with dread both night and day, never sure of your life. In the morning you will say, 'If only it were evening!' and in the evening, 'If only it were morning!'– because of the terror that will fill your hearts and the sights that your eyes will see.        (Deut. 28.65-67)

I will bring you from the nations and gather you from the countries where you have been scattered – with a mighty hand and an outstretched arm and with outpoured wrath. I will bring you into the wilderness of the nations and there, face to face, I will execute judgment upon you. As I judged your ancestors in the wilderness of the land of Egypt, so I will judge you, declares the Sovereign LORD.        (Ezek. 20.34-36)

There is, however, another possible answer to these questions. One of the most unusual and yet significant stories in the Old Testament is that of Job, a man mightily blessed by God, and yet allowed to undergo a series of punishing tests, instigated by Satan, in order prove his faithfulness. This testing becomes almost worse than death itself and causes Job to question God's nature at the deepest level. However, through all this, Job's response is astonishing: he continues to worship God (Job 1.21) and despite the worsening situation and his own intense wrestling with God, declares that 'Though he slay me *yet* I will hope in him' (13.15). His deepest longing is to see God face to face (19.25-27), a wish that is finally granted him, and in the end he receives a blessing twice the level that he originally enjoyed.

At face value, there is nothing in Job's story that would provide a direct and explicit link to the sufferings of the Jewish people collectively through history. However, there is one passage in the Bible that might cause us to investigate this further, and for this we need to turn to the New Testament.

In Revelation Chapter 12, a remarkable sequence of images appears. We see a woman in labour, clothed with the sun, wearing a crown of twelve stars and with the moon under her feet, who gives birth to a child who is to rule the nations with an iron sceptre. A seven-headed dragon tries to devour the child as it is born, but it is snatched up to the throne of God. Enraged, the dragon pursues the woman instead, who flees into the wilderness.

Although much of Revelation is difficult to unravel, this particular set of images is not hard to decode. In the Old Testament, Israel is sometimes depicted as a woman in labour,[1] and the reference to the sun, moon and twelve stars clearly links back to the Jewish nation in its original form, as depicted in Joseph's dream in Genesis 37.9-10. The child destined to rule the nations almost certainly refers to the Messiah, borrowing imagery from Psalm 2.8-9 and Isaiah 9.6, while the dragon is Satan himself, as verse 9 makes clear.

Along with chapters 1 and 2 of Job, this is one of a relatively small number of places in scripture in which Satan takes centre stage, and both accounts are almost unique in describing his interaction with other angels. Both also show clearly how events in heaven can have a direct consequence on the earth. In either case God is clearly in ultimate control but Satan appears to be pulling the strings. In Job we see how a series of apparently unrelated and inexplicable disasters, which occur in an observable pattern, betray Satan's unseen influence behind the scenes. In a similar way, history shows us a remarkable and chilling pattern to attacks on the Jewish nation over many centuries.

Even the most hardened sceptics find it difficult to explain away an extraordinary series of coincidences on one particular date in the Jewish religious calendar: the 9th of Av. It was on this date that the First Temple was destroyed by the Babylonians in 586 BC. On the same date the Romans destroyed the Second Temple in 70 AD, resulting in about a million deaths. Exactly the same date marks the ending of the Bar Kokhba revolt in 135 AD, with the loss of more than 500,000 lives.

Within a couple of days on either side, a series of catastrophes in the Middle Ages line up with this very same point in the calendar: the expulsion of Jews from England in 1290, from France in 1306 and from Spain in 1492. Even in the twentieth century the pattern continues: on this very date Germany entered World War One, beginning the countdown that led ultimately to the horrors of the Holocaust. Likewise the same day saw Himmler receive authorisation in 1941 for the 'Final Solution', and the first deportations of Jews from the Warsaw Ghetto to the Treblinka Concentration Camp in 1942.

Before the idea of linking all these events is ruled out of court as yet another wild conspiracy theory, it is worth reminding ourselves that lunar calendar used by the Jews runs out of phase with any other dating system. It is extremely unlikely that any secular power could stage-manage such a series of disasters even if it wanted to. However hard it might be for us to accept with our modern sceptical worldview, it simply beggars belief that so many calamities on this date could be pure coincidence. It bears all the hallmarks of something far more sinister. Are we, then, seeing, as with Job, the outlines of a co-ordinated spiritual attack?[2]

The passage in Revelation continues as follows:

The woman was given the two wings of a great eagle, so that she might fly to the place prepared for her in the wilderness, where she would be taken care of for a time, times and half a time, out of the snake's reach. Then from his mouth the snake spewed water like a river, to overtake the woman and sweep her away with the torrent. But the earth helped the woman by opening its mouth and swallowing the river that the dragon had spewed out of his mouth. (12.14-16)

In these verses there appears to be a restriction on what Satan can achieve, just as we see in Job, where Satan is instructed to preserve Job's life at all costs, even though everything else is taken away. This might remind us of the way that, despite centuries of persecution, the Jewish people have survived and even flourished, keeping their culture intact against all the odds. In 1899 Mark Twain observed in *Harper's Magazine*:

If the statistics are right, the Jews constitute but one percent of the human race. It suggests a nebulous dim puff of star dust lost in the blaze of the Milky Way. Properly the Jew ought hardly be heard of; but he is heard of, has always been heard of.

He is as prominent on the planet as any other people, and his commercial importance is extravagantly out of proportion to the smallness of his bulk. His contributions to the world's list of great names in literature, science, art, music, finance, medicine, and abstruse learning are also way out of proportion to the weakness of his numbers. He has made a marvelous fight in this world, in all ages; and has done it with his hands tied behind him. He could be vain of himself, and be excused for it.

The Egyptian, the Babylonian, and the Persian, rose, filled the planet with sound and splendor, then faded to dream-stuff and passed away; the Greek and the Roman followed, and made a vast noise, and they are gone; other peoples have sprung up and held their torch high for a time, but it burned out, and they sit in twilight now, or have vanished.

The Jew saw them all, beat them all, and is now what he always was, exhibiting no decadence, no infirmities of age, no weakening of his parts, no slowing of his energies, no dulling of his alert and aggressive mind. All things are mortal but the Jew;

all other forces pass, but he remains. What is the secret of his immortality?[3]

Tolstoy wrote similarly in 1891 that:

A Jew is a sacred being who procured an eternal fire from the heavens and with it illuminated the earth and those who live on it. He is the spring and the source from which the rest of the nations drew their religions and beliefs. ... The nation which neither slaughter nor torture could exterminate, which neither fire nor sword of civilizations were able to erase from the face of earth, the nation which first proclaimed the word of the Lord, the nation which preserved the prophecy for so long and passed it on to the rest of humanity, such a nation cannot vanish.

A Jew is eternal; he is an embodiment of eternity.[4]

One extraordinary indicator of this remarkable preservation of Jewish culture in the unlikeliest of situations can be found in the Lemba people who live in Zimbabwe and South Africa. Tribal tradition claims that their ancestors emigrated from Israel about 2,500 years ago. Scientific studies of the tribe have shown that fifty per cent of males carry the Jewish priestly gene.[5] They discourage marriage outside the tribe, they do not eat pork or the blood of animals, they observe the Sabbath, they practise male circumcision, they perform ritual slaughter of their animals, and are divided into twelve sub-tribes. They also possess something equivalent to the Ark of the Covenant known as the *ngoma lungundu*. Considered to be too holy to be touched, only the hereditary priesthood of the tribe are permitted to carry it, using poles inserted into rings on either side. The survival and preservation of such a group so far from their original homeland over so many centuries is difficult to explain in purely human terms.

Furthermore, Mark Twain's observation about the disproportionate influence Jewish people exert in relation to their numbers is even more true today, well over a century after he made his remarks. Given that Jews today make up a tiny fraction of the world's population - less than one quarter of one per cent - it is extraordinary to note that, out of all Nobel prizes awarded since 1901, Jews have won a total of 22% of awards given, including 38% in economics,[6] 26% in medicine, 26% in physics, 21% in chemistry, 13% in literature and 9% of the peace prizes.[7] Between 1905 and 1936 they won 37% of all the Nobel prizes awarded to German citizens. Since *La Grande Médaille de l'Académie des Sciences de France*, France's top scientific honour, was instituted in 1997, Jews have won no less than 50% of all awards given.[8] And worldwide, Jews constitute 11.5% of the world's billionaires, rising to 40% in the United States.[9]

I would challenge anyone who believes that the Jews no longer enjoy special favour with God to provide a plausible explanation for this disparity, outside God's promise to Abraham that 'all peoples on earth will be blessed through you' (Gen. 12.3). Just as the curse on Levi and the scattering of his descendants becomes the means through which God blesses the nation as a whole through the Mosaic priesthood, so too the scattering of Israel through the nations seems to have become the means by which he has blessed the entire world, fulfilling the promise in Isaiah

27.6 that 'in days to come Jacob will take root, Israel will bud and blossom and fill all the world with fruit.'

Behind the history of the Jewish nation, then, we can see two hands at work. As we saw in Chapter Three, it was God who selected Israel out of all the nations of the earth to represent him and be his witnesses. Through Israel his law would be declared, his power would be demonstrated on earth and ultimately the Messiah, the child described in Revelation 12, would be born. And throughout centuries of dispersal, fragmentation and persecution God has preserved them for a final regathering in the Holy Land, just as he always promised.

But we also see a more sinister hand at work, with Satan desperate at all costs either to wipe the Jewish people from the face of the earth. The fact that he is depicted as a seven-headed dragon in Revelation suggests that there are a number of avenues through which such attacks could arise. We know of course, of many such attacks from the Bible itself, going back to Exodus. A classic example is Haman's declaration in the book of Esther:

Then Haman said to King Xerxes, 'There is a certain people dispersed among the peoples in all the provinces of your kingdom who keep themselves separate. Their customs are different from those of all other people, and they do not obey the king's laws; it is not in the king's best interest to tolerate them.

(Esther 3.8)

As we have seen, such attacks have continued throughout history, spanning the ages from Haman, to Herod, to Hitler, to Hamas in our own day. If we compare Haman's words with what Voltaire wrote many centuries later, for example, it is possible to see the same fundamental spirit at work:

We find in [Jews] only an ignorant and barbarous people, who have long united the most sordid avarice with the most detestable superstition and the most invincible hatred for every people by whom they are tolerated and enriched.

We might not, however, be wholly surprised to see such similar sentiments coming from a power-hungry egotist like Haman or someone who disdained the Bible as much as Voltaire. It is particularly disturbing, however, to see so-called *Christians* playing such a large role in denigrating, humiliating and at times even destroying the Jewish people. Did the church unwittingly allow itself to become a further channel for much of this destructive venom, effectively doing Satan's work for him? And why have the Jews in particular borne the brunt of such attacks?

Could it be that by driving an increasing wedge between Judaism and the church Satan is actually trying to prevent Jesus' return, or to or postpone it indefinitely? Might the return of Christ actually be *dependent* on the Jewish people accepting him as Messiah (given his remark that 'you will not see me again **until** you say, "Blessed is he who comes in the name of the Lord"' [Matt.23.39])?

If so, 'replacement theology' is an 'own goal' of colossal proportions. And its consequences are far-reaching: not only has it driven the Jews further from their Messiah, but it has caused the church to develop in a vacuum, orphaned from its original family. How easily we have forgotten that for the early church there was no such thing as the 'Old'

Testament: it was their Bible pure and simple, from which Paul drew the great doctrines of justification by faith and deliverance through the cross. Yet for many Christians, it has now become like a forbidding, dimly-lit museum - to be visited rarely (with the possible exception of the Psalms) - and only out of a sense of duty.

Some Christians would choose to go further. For them the Old Testament's tales of carnage, genocide and obscure rituals seem completely alien to our modern age, and the God who presides over them appears angry and unforgiving, in contrast to the loving Father that Jesus revealed. This cruel caricature ignores the fact that the New Testament is far more theologically 'challenging' in its description of hell, predestination and individual judgment than anything in the Old.

Such a view of the Old Testament as outdated and cancelled out by the New comes precariously close to the Muslim doctrine of 'abrogation', where a later revelation in the Qur'an can override an earlier one. It would be better for proponents of such beliefs to come clean and say openly that the Old Testament's view of the future is actually wrong: there was never to be a future restoration of Israel, and the promises made are null and void. As we pointed out in Chapter One, such an outlook is not far removed from that of the second century heretic Marcion, who discarded the Old Testament as the work of an inferior deity, incapable of the lofty heights scaled in the writings of Paul.

It is, of course, Satan's purpose throughout history to twist scripture and misapply it for his own purposes, stealing the glory rightly due to God alone. But we need to be aware of his schemes. We ignore scripture or misdirect it at our own peril. All too often the church has simply prised scriptures out of context and used them as weapons. Religious fanaticism without a true baptism of love can be a deadly missile in Satan's hands. A story from the gospels illustrates this well:

And he sent messengers on ahead, who went into a Samaritan village to get things ready for him; but the people there did not welcome him, because he was heading for Jerusalem. When the disciples James and John saw this, they asked, 'Lord, do you want us to call fire down from heaven to destroy them[1]?' But Jesus turned and rebuked them. (Luke 9.52-55)

Many later manuscripts of the New Testament report Jesus saying here, '*You do not know what manner of spirit you are of*'. While these words are absent from the earliest surviving versions of the Gospel, their fundamental insight is likely to be correct.

In the book of Job, his so-called friends are convinced that they are right, unaware that it is their own distorted theological outlook and accusing spirit that motivates them. Neither Job, his wife, or his so-called friends have even the slightest inkling that it is Satan who is the instigator of Job's misfortunes. The friends, convinced that Job has reaped his own fate, launch an ever-increasing tide of invective against him, little realising that they are actually doing Satan's work for him!

If I may be forgiven a rather provocative analogy, Job's three friends are not unlike the three main branches of the

Christian church, Catholic, Orthodox and Protestant, who, as we saw in Chapter Two, have all resolutely maintained through much of history that the Jews bear responsibility for their own downfall through their rebellion against God. The 'friends', of course, are then elbowed out of the way by the rather arrogant young upstart Elihu (cue the charismatics!) who points out that they have all got it completely wrong, before proceeding to repeat exactly what the others have already said in slightly different words.

In the end, they all discover - inevitably to their great astonishment - that when God finally shows his face, it is *they* who need Job's prayers, not vice versa. Does this story have anything to say to the church throughout history? Are we the ones who are actually in the dock?

And what about the longer-term consequences of our actions? In the parable of the sheep and the goats in Matthew 25, Jesus says, 'Truly, I say to you, as you did it to one of the least of these my brothers, you did it to me' (v. 40 ESV), with consequences that are eternal in scope. Who does Jesus mean by his 'brothers' here?

The most obvious and probable answer, of course, is that it refers to any true believer. This ties in well with what Jesus says in Matthew 12.50, that 'whoever does the will of my Father in heaven is my brother and sister and mother.'

But, given that the gospel at its outset names Jesus as 'Son of David' and 'King of the Jews', and that Joseph is told to name him Jesus 'because he *will* save *his people* from their sins' (1.21), we should not entirely dismiss the possibility of applying the word 'brothers' to his fellow Jews specifically, a view advanced by some theologians arguing from a dispensational viewpoint.[10] Although this may seem to hang on a slender thread of logic, it might become more plausible when we see how many Old Testament passages concerning Israel are echoed at the beginning of the parable (verses 31-32):

> When the Son of Man *comes in his glory*, and *all the angels with him*, then he will *sit on his glorious throne*. Before him will be *gathered all the nations* ... (ESV)

The words in italics here recall three Old Testament passages in particular, and in each one Yahweh himself appears in judgement to defend his people Israel. One of these is from Zechariah 14, which describes how the Lord will come to deliver Jerusalem from enemy attack:

> I will *gather all the nations* to Jerusalem to fight against it ... Then the LORD will go out and fight against those nations, as he fights on a day of battle. ... Then the LORD my God *will come, and all the holy ones with him.* (Zech. 14.2, 3, 5)

Another is Psalm 102, which tells of how God rescues his people:

> *But you, LORD, sit enthroned for ever*; ...
> You will arise and have compassion on Zion,
>   for it is time to show favour to her;
>   the appointed time has come.
>
> *The nations will fear the name of the LORD,*
>   all the kings of the earth will revere your glory.

For the LORD will rebuild Zion
*and appear in his glory.* (Ps. 102.12, 13, 15-16)

A third is from chapter 3 of Joel, which again describes God's judgement on those nations who attack Israel:

'I will *gather all nations*
   and bring them down to the Valley of Jehoshaphat.
There I will put them on trial
   for what they did to my inheritance, my people Israel,
because they scattered my people among the nations
   and divided up my land. ...
'Let the nations be roused;
   let them advance into the Valley of Jehoshaphat,
for *there I will sit*
   *to judge all the nations on every side.*' (Joel 3:2, 12)

Moreover, verse 40 itself ("Truly, I say to you, as you did it to one of the least of these my brothers, you did it to me" [ESV]) also recalls Old Testament passages where God treats what happens to Israel as being directed to himself personally. For instance, in Zechariah 2.8 he says,

'whoever touches you *touches the apple of my eye.*'

Similarly, Joel 3 verses 2 and 4 says:

'They cast lots for my people  ...
   *Are you repaying me for something I have done?* If you are
paying me back, I will swiftly and speedily return on your own
heads what you have done.'

Even if, as the vast majority of scholars would argue, Israel were not the primary focus of Matthew 25, the warning from the Old Testament passages it recalls seems to be clear. One of the measures of God's judgement will be how we have treated the Jewish people:

'You should not gloat over your brother
    in the day of his misfortune,
nor rejoice over the people of Judah
    in the day of their destruction,
nor boast so much
    in the day of their trouble. ...
'The day of the LORD is near
    for all nations.
*As you have done, it will be done to you;*
    *your deeds will return upon your own head.*' (Ob. 12, 15)

Although this passage is directed at Edom, it surely has ramifications for the church today, as does a similar warning from Ezekiel:

'Because you harboured an ancient hostility and delivered the Israelites over to the sword at the time of their calamity, the time their punishment reached its climax, therefore as surely as I live, declares the Sovereign LORD, *I will give you over to bloodshed and it will pursue you. Since you did not hate bloodshed, bloodshed will pursue you.*' (Ezek. 35.5-6)

Anti-Semitism may manifest in various forms, whether it is an unashamed out-and-out attack or merely a subtle 'twisting' of scripture, but its source is always the same, as are its consequences. We reap what we have sown. In Esther, for example, the very gallows that Haman designs to destroy Mordecai proves to be the instrument of his own destruction.

Too often the church has failed to learn from the repeated consequences of its actions. In Chapter Two, for example, we pointed out that in 694 the Seventeenth Council of Toledo required all Jews in what is now Spain to be sold into slavery, with their property confiscated, and have their children over the age of seven forcibly removed and educated in monasteries. Within twenty years Spain had capitulated completely to Islam (under which, it has to be said, the Jews received dramatically better treatment). Similarly, the Russian church was complicit in numerous pogroms of Jews in the early years of the twentieth century in which thousands lost their lives. Once more, within twenty years the Revolution had come and the Orthodox Church found itself subject to a crushing atheist government. Coincidence - maybe? But it should certainly cause us to reflect.

Considered against this background, the end of Revelation 12 contains a very stark warning to the church. When the dragon's plans to destroy the woman are thwarted, he changes tack:

Then the dragon was enraged at the woman and went off to wage war against the rest of her offspring – those who keep God's commands and hold fast their testimony about Jesus. (v. 17)

In other words, its next target is *the Christians*! Already today we see Christians in many parts of the world experiencing unparalleled levels of persecution. Such attacks are occurring on a greater scale than at any other time in church history, and many bear an uncanny similarity to the way that so-called 'Christians' have treated their Jewish counterparts in the past. If we do not stand up for our Jewish brothers and sisters, who will stand up for us?

We have already acknowledged the colossal *faux pas* made by the Jewish people when in large measure they rejected their Messiah. But has not the treatment of the Jews by the church been a mistake of similar magnitude? All we have done is to drive an ever greater wedge between Jesus and the fellow countrymen he came to save. Just as the religious authorities in Jerusalem who conspired to put Jesus to death mistakenly thought they were performing God's will, the church has fallen victim to the same kind of scam, which originates ultimately from the pit of hell.

It is in this light that a re-examination of 'replacement theology' is long overdue. It is based on a faulty reading of scripture and has led indirectly to incalculable suffering throughout history. Most of all, it has driven the Jews ever further from their Messiah. The time has come to redress the balance: to restore the Old Testament to its rightful place alongside the New, and reassess the relationship between Israel and the church.

Many today, however, will argue passionately for a different viewpoint. They will point out (rightly) the radical change of direction in the New Testament, in that God's relationship to mankind has been changed irreversibly through the cross. The conclusion that they draw from this is that the Jews no longer hold a special or privileged place in God's designs because his focus is now on something indescribably greater - to reach every nation on earth.

So were the promises that God gave to Israel in the Old Testament overturned by something infinitely greater still - the death and resurrection of Jesus? Is physical Israel now superfluous to God's plans? Four writers in particular are often cited as advancing such a view: Matthew, Luke, John and Paul. In the next three chapters, we will begin investigating their writings, to see whether a real case can be made for arguing that the church, not the Jewish people, are now the new 'Israel of God'.

# 5 RECONSIDERING MATTHEW

At first sight, Matthew's gospel seems to make an excellent case for 'replacement theology'. Much in Jesus' teaching and actions appears to overturn radically the existing *status quo*. New wineskins, overturned tables, a withered tree, mountains cast into the sea, evicted tenants - all seem to point to radical break with the past and the switch to a completely new order of things.

Several parables seem to direct the heat onto the nation of Israel itself. A clear example is the story of the tenants in the vineyard (21.33-44), whose symbolism many of Jesus' listeners would have recognised. Isaiah chapter 5 likened the nation of Israel to a vineyard with the owner as God himself. Because it produced bad fruit, the vineyard was to be trampled down and destroyed.

As Jesus tells it, however, the story has a new twist. When the time for harvest arrives and the owner attempts to collect some fruit, the servants that he sends are killed and maimed by those leasing the vineyard. As a last resort the owner decides to send his son, hoping for a better response. But the tenants seize the opportunity, putting him to death so that they can lay hold of the inheritance for themselves. As a result, the owner destroys the tenants and rents the vineyard out to others, who 'will give him his share of the crop at harvest time' (v. 41). Jesus' conclusion is blunt: 'the kingdom of God will be *taken away from you* and *given to a people* who will produce its fruit' (v. 43).

It might be natural to conclude from this that God had finally finished with Israel and was about transfer his blessings to others. Certainly this is how the story has often been understood.

Jesus goes on to give another parable about a king who gives a wedding-feast for his son (22.1-14). Here the invited guests ignore their invitations and some attack and kill the messengers who sent them. As a result, the king sends troops to kill those to whom invitations were sent and to set their town on fire. A whole set of new guests are then invited in their place. Again, this sounds decidedly like a replacement list!

These stories seem to throw light on two striking actions which take place shortly beforehand. Visiting the temple, Jesus causes a commotion by turning over the tables of the money-changers (21.12). After this he goes on to curse a fig tree that has produced no fruit, and it withers instantly

(21.18-22). The message in each case appears to be the same: the old order is being violently replaced, and a new order will come in its stead.

The warning to the Jewish nation is scarcely disguised. While neither of these parables is unique to Matthew's gospel (they both appear in Luke and, except for the wedding-feast story, also in Mark), the particular way he handles them seems to highlight the impression that God's favours are about to be withdrawn, and that violent consequences will result.

A still stronger rebuke appears in Jesus' words to the Gentile centurion in Matthew Chapter 8. Commending him for his courage in believing what would normally be considered impossible, Jesus says,

'Truly I tell you, I have not found anyone in Israel with such great faith. I say to you that many will come from the east and the west, and will take their places at the feast with Abraham, Isaac and Jacob in the kingdom of heaven. *But the subjects of the kingdom will be thrown outside*, into the darkness, where there will be weeping and gnashing of teeth.' (8.10-12).

At first sight this seems absolute and final: *all* the subjects of the kingdom, which we would naturally presume to be Israel, will be thrown out. No scope appears to be left for exceptions of any kind.

These warnings seem to come to a head in the fierceness of Jesus' denunciation of the Pharisees and the teachers of the law in Matthew 23, which finally widens to judgement on a whole generation:

'Woe to you, teachers of the law and Pharisees, you hypocrites! You build tombs for the prophets and decorate the graves of the righteous. And you say, "If we had lived in the days of our ancestors, we would not have taken part with them in shedding the blood of the prophets." So you testify against yourselves that you are the descendants of those who murdered the prophets. Go ahead, then, and complete what your ancestors started!

'You snakes! You brood of vipers! How will you escape being condemned to hell? Therefore I am sending you prophets and sages and teachers. Some of them you will kill and crucify; others you will flog in your synagogues and pursue from town to town. And so upon you will come all the righteous blood that has been shed on earth, from the blood of righteous Abel to the blood of Zechariah son of Berekiah, whom you murdered between the temple and the altar. Truly I tell you, all this will come upon this generation.' (vv. 29-36)

The tone of this seems to be answered by the events which follow later. After Pilate disowns the action he is about to authorise by washing his hands in front of the crowd, the multitudes cry out, 'His blood is on us and on our children!' (Matt. 27.25). Matthew appears to want us to be in no doubt as to who must shoulder the greatest blame for Jesus' death.

All these examples would appear at first sight to provide strong support for the idea that Israel is finished in God's purposes. According to this reading of Matthew, Jesus is serving final warning on the Jewish nation that God is planning to judge and replace it. As with the fate which awaited the inhabitants of the earth before the flood, there is no way back. God's judgement is final and irreversible.

Persuasive though it might seem at first, however, this view does not stand up to closer scrutiny. Such an interpretation completely overlooks Matthew's clear purposes from the outset. While individual segments might suggest certain conclusions, reading the gospel as a connected whole creates a very different impression.

To begin with, it soon becomes obvious that Matthew's gospel is by far the most openly Jewish of the four. Far from overturning his Jewish heritage, his over-arching theme appears to be that Jesus is 'King of the Jews', a fact emphasised both at his birth and at his death (2.2, 27.37). To illustrate this, he begins by showing Jesus' descent from Abraham as the rightful descendant of the throne of David. Joseph is told to name him Jesus 'because he will save *his people* from their sins' (1.21), and by combining this with the description from Micah just ten verses later of a 'a ruler who *will* shepherd *my people Israel*' (2.6) Matthew seems to hint that the promised salvation is intended in the first place primarily for the Jewish people themselves.

Matthew is keen to further underline the specifically Jewish nature of Jesus' mission. He is sent to 'the lost sheep of Israel' and directs his disciples away from Gentile or Samaritan areas as a result (Matt. 10.5-6). The Gentiles, by contrast, are merely 'the dogs' who 'eat the crumbs that fall from their master's table' (15.27). Far from being purely a temporary arrangement, he tells them, 'you will not finish going through the towns of Israel before the Son of Man comes' (Matt. 10.23). And in the age to come, the disciples will be judging not Gentile nations but 'the twelve tribes of Israel' (Matt. 19.28).

Against this background, even the so-called 'last commission' at the end of the gospel, to 'go and make disciples of all nations' (28.19) appears not to be a radical realignment of God's purposes, but simply an expansion of one of the verses from Isaiah that we noted in Chapter Three:

'It is too light a thing that you should ... bring back the preserved of Israel;
I will make you as a light for the nations,
    that my salvation may reach to the end of the earth.'

(49.6 ESV)

In other respects, also, Matthew is anxious to build on the heritage of the Old Testament. He makes repeated attempts to show how different aspects of Jesus' life fulfil Old Testament prophecy. He quotes Jesus as saying that he has come not to abolish the Law or the Prophets but to fulfil them (Matt. 5.17), and continues with the following statement:

'For truly I tell you, until heaven and earth disappear, not the smallest letter, not the least stroke of a pen, will by any means disappear from the Law until everything is accomplished.'

(v. 18)

In many respects, Matthew models his picture of Jesus on Moses, who is rescued at birth from a cruel, despotic king, spends formative years in Egypt, leads his people to freedom through mighty signs and wonders and gives them a new law on the mountain-top. His violent actions in the temple make sense if we consider those of Moses in passing judgement on the idolatrous worship of a golden calf, and his death marks the ultimate fulfilment of the Jewish Passover, opening the way into a Promised Land.

It seems clear, then, that Matthew's Gospel was written with a Jewish audience in mind. Why, otherwise, is it only in Matthew that we find the expectation that Jesus' followers will continue to make offerings in the temple (5.23-4)? Why, in 15.1-20, a passage which appears to be based closely on Mark Chapter 7.1-23, does Matthew pointedly omit Mark's statement, 'Jesus declared all foods clean' (7.19)? Could it be that his original readers were still following kosher dietary laws? And why, alone of the gospel writers, does he quote Jesus' warning to the disciples to 'Pray that your flight will not take place ... on the Sabbath' (Matt. 24.20) - a statement that makes little sense outside of a Jewish context?

Most significant, perhaps, is a verse from chapter 18:

If he refuses to listen to them, tell it to the church. And if he refuses to listen even to the church, let him be to you as a Gentile and a tax collector. (Matt. 18.17)

It is striking here that, in one of only two passages mentioning the word 'church' in any of the gospels, Matthew quotes Jesus as using the word 'Gentiles' to describe those *outside* it. Could it be that Jesus is conceiving of the church in primarily *Jewish* terms?[1]

With this in mind, we can re-read the passages discussed before through different eyes. On more careful inspection, what we see is Jesus attacking the hypocrisy and complacency of the religious hierarchy, not the nation as a whole.

For example, while the parable of the wicked tenants sounds like a final judgement on the entire Jewish nation, Matthew actually concludes,

When the chief priests and the Pharisees heard his parables, they perceived that he was *speaking about them*. (Matt. 21.45 ESV)

Similarly, the 'invited guests' in the parable of the wedding banquet are not the Jewish people as a whole, since those who attend subsequently are others from the same city (22.9-10). The hint is once more that the invited guests are the religious leaders and the well-to-do: in Luke's version it is 'the poor, the crippled, the blind and the lame' who receive the second set of invitations (14.21).

What Jesus seems to be attacking in these parables, therefore, is not the Jewish nation as such, but rather the special privileges zealously guarded by a religious elite unwilling to listen to God's appointed spokesmen, and who bolster their position by marginalising the 'outsiders'. It is these outcasts from *within* Judaism, such as the tax collectors and the prostitutes mentioned immediately beforehand in 21.31-32, that God wants to call up to take their place.

This hardly gives succour to the church who, for many centuries, has tightly guarded these 'special privileges' for herself and marginalised the 'unclean' Jews who became, by an ironic reversal, the dogs who eat the crumbs from under their master's table! Nothing could be further from the thrust of Jesus' radical message. Far from predicting the end of God's dealings with the Jews, Jesus is attacking the very exclusivism that the church has so willingly embraced.

So what are we to make of Chapter 8 of Matthew, with its apparently absolute declaration that the 'subjects of the kingdom' will be thrown into outer darkness?

Firstly, we need to recognise that Jesus sometimes made uncompromising statements for their shock value. Where he tells us to 'hate our father and mother' or to 'cut off' our hand if it causes us to sin, he is using extreme language to underline the cost of discipleship. It is only when we look at the wider context of these sayings that we begin to understand what he really means by them.

In this respect, we should remember that many similarly final-sounding pronouncements are made by Yahweh himself in the Old Testament. In Hosea 1.9, for example, God calls Israel 'Not My People', and then completely reverses his stance in the following verse!

Again and again, in God's sovereign plan, grace and mercy ultimately prevail over the strict outworking of justice. The same is surely true here: later in Matthew, Jesus says to Jerusalem that 'you will not see me again *until* you say, "Blessed is he who comes in the name of the Lord."'(23.39). Could it be, therefore, that Jesus is prophesying the events of the church age, and a temporary exile *until* 'the renewal of all things, when the Son of Man sits on his glorious throne', when the disciples will reign over a restored Israel (Matt. 19.28)?[2]

In any case we need to establish who Jesus means by the 'subjects [literally, "sons"] of the kingdom'. In his other parables those who *regard themselves* as the rightful subjects are the ones whose place is least secure. By contrast, it is the ones outside the pale to whom the good news is directed: the prostitutes, the tax-collectors, the lepers, the unclean, the blind and the lame.

And that leads us to the final and most important point: reading the story from our perspective today, what is the warning to us? As the church, *we* are also subjects of the kingdom. Do we really have the faith the centurion has? And if not, what will become of us?

I would like to suggest that this is the crux of the matter. The story is not primarily about Jews and Gentiles but about someone with an extravagant faith, because he fully understands the principle of delegated authority. The secular 'outsider' understands this perfectly - the religious 'insiders' do not.

Alas, the same problem is true of much of today's church. By and large, we have lost the certainty of faith and the ability to use the God-given authority which so animates the church in the book of Acts. Far too often, today's Western church greets reports of miracles with suspicion rather than thanksgiving and expectancy. All too frequently, an influential educated elite looks down on the child-like faith of those too whole-hearted to share their carefully worked-out theology of doubt. If the thrust of Jesus' warning at the end is against the religious complacency that automatically belongs to a privileged group, we as the church should be very concerned.

What of the harsh warnings to the Pharisees in Matthew 23? The fact that Jesus warns that they will 'flog' those who believe the gospel in *synagogues* suggests that he is focusing his remarks on their treatment of *fellow Jews* alone. Jesus is engaging in a vigorous debate *within* Judaism rather than *against* it.

In fact, Jesus is not alone in his observations on the Pharisees. His Jewish contemporary, Philo, agrees that they could be 'merciless' towards those who broke the law,[3] though he is probably directing his remarks at the disciples of Rabbi Shammai, rather than the more lenient followers of Hillel, influential teachers both active shortly before the lifetime of Jesus.

In many ways, the warnings that Jesus gives are probably no more severe than those delivered by Yahweh to the principal men of Israel in passages such as Ezekiel 34:

'Woe to you shepherds of Israel who only take care of yourselves! Should not shepherds take care of the flock? You eat the curds, clothe yourselves with the wool and slaughter the choice animals, but you do not take care of the flock. You have not strengthened the weak or healed those who are ill or bound up the injured. You have not brought back the strays or searched for the lost. You have ruled them harshly and brutally. ... I am against the shepherds and will hold them accountable for my flock. I will remove them from tending the flock so that the shepherds can no longer feed themselves. I will rescue my flock from their mouths, and it will no longer be food for them.'

(Ezek. 34.2-4, 10)

In both cases a sharp distinction is being made between the nation's religious leaders and the people they purport to lead. God's commitment to Israel itself remains unwavering.

This leaves us with the one verse in Matthew which has caused more problems for the Jews than perhaps any other in the Bible. Matthew 27.25 says that 'all the people answered, "His blood is on us and on our children!"'. Again and again, this phrase has been used to justify countless acts of barbarity towards the Jewish people.

Certainly, at face value, the phrase can be taken to mean exactly what it implies: when Paul is rejected by the Corinthian Jews he cries out:

'Your blood be on your own heads! I am innocent of it. From now on I will go to the Gentiles.' (Acts 18.6)

However, it is quite possible that Matthew is trying to explain the background to the destruction of Jerusalem in AD 70, and that by 'all the people' he is referring simply to the inhabitants of Jerusalem itself (compare Acts 13.27). This clearly recalls the words of Jeremiah, who, when 'all the people' in Jerusalem demand that he be put to death (Jer. 26.8), replies:

'Only know for certain that if you put me to death, *you will bring innocent blood upon yourselves and upon this city and its inhabitants*, for in truth the LORD sent me to you to speak all these words in your ears.' (v. 15 ESV)

However great the warning of severe judgement here, it falls well short of suggesting an abandonment of the entire nation by God.

But it is also conceivable that Matthew has something deeper in mind here. The timing of the statement, in the middle of the Passover Festival, is highly relevant. Here 'all the people' pronounce the blood of Jesus over themselves and their families. In Exodus 12, '*all the members* of the community of Israel' slaughter the Passover lamb and place its blood over the door of each house. But in Egypt the blood does not spell out judgement - it points to protection and deliverance (v. 6-7)!

By making the Jews (rather than the Romans) largely responsible for Jesus' death, it may well be, therefore, that Matthew is trying to bring out its redemptive Passover significance. Since he quotes earlier in his gospel part of Isaiah 53, he would surely have been familiar with its continuation:

yet we considered him punished by God,
   stricken by him, and afflicted.
But he was pierced for our transgressions,
   he was crushed for our iniquities;
*the punishment that brought us peace was on him,*
   *and by his wounds we are healed.* (vv. 4-5)

What should we conclude? Matthew's gospel, though clearly lambasting the religious leadership of Israel, can in no way be described as anti-Jewish. Far from rejecting his people, Matthew writes as a Jew keen to show Jesus as the fulfilment of everything that the Jewish nation stands for.

Indeed, Matthew seems eager to demonstrate, like Paul in Ephesians, how Gentiles and Jews can be *joint* heirs in Christ. Why, otherwise, should he draw such attention to notable Gentiles, such as Rahab and Ruth, in Jesus' family tree? Why should it be *Gentiles* who are first to recognise Jesus as 'King of the Jews'? Why should he include two feeding miracles, one in a Jewish area and one in a Gentile area? And, at a deeper symbolic level, why should he have Jesus healing *two* demoniacs and *two* blind men in places where the other gospels mention only one?

If so, the warnings in Matthew's gospel against the religious leadership are just as applicable to us today. Have we, like them, become complacent and arrogant? Do we, too, face judgement over our treatment of the weak and marginalised? And could such judgement even extend to how the church and the nations have treated the Jewish people generally? Perhaps we should at least consider the possibility that, as we suggested before, Jesus' words in Matthew 25, "Truly I tell you, whatever you did for one of the least of these *brothers and sisters* of mine, you did for me", could be applied specifically to the way we treat his fellow Jews themselves.

It is perhaps worth concluding with a verse from earlier in Matthew's Gospel:

'So if you are offering your gift at the altar and there remember that your brother has something against you, leave your gift there before the altar and go. First be reconciled to your brother, and then come and offer your gift.' (5.23-24 ESV)

Is this not *precisely* what the church, in all its various branches and denominations, needs to do right now?

# 6 RECONSIDERING LUKE

Although the gospels of Matthew and Luke share a great deal in common, there are some significant differences in emphasis. Unlike Matthew, Luke seems to have tailored his work to a largely Gentile audience. Gone is the emphasis on a purely Jewish mission that dominates much of Matthew - for Luke Israel seems to be simply the first staging-post for something much wider.

This can be seen in their different approaches to Jesus' ancestry. While Matthew's genealogy demonstrates Jesus' impeccable Jewish pedigree and his rightful succession to the royal bloodline of Israel, Luke's family tree traces a rather different route right back to Adam himself, the universal fount of humanity.

Perhaps for this reason, Luke misses out the story of the Syro-Phoenician woman that appears in Matthew and Mark, with its disparaging reference to Gentiles as 'dogs' who eat the crumbs from under their master's table. Instead, he shows Jesus arousing rage in his home town of Nazareth by pointing out how God on occasions treated Gentiles more favourably than Jews in the Old Testament:

'I assure you that there were many widows in Israel in Elijah's time, when the sky was shut for three and a half years and there was a severe famine throughout the land. Yet Elijah was not sent to any of them, but to a widow in Zarephath in the region of Sidon. And there were many in Israel with leprosy in the time of Elisha the prophet, yet not one of them was cleansed – only Naaman the Syrian.' (Luke 4.25-27)

Alongside the parables of the tenants in the vineyard and the guests at the wedding feast that we noted in Matthew's gospel, Luke includes other material that might also suggest that Israel's days as God's chosen people are numbered. One such story is the following:

Then he told this parable: 'A man had a fig-tree growing in his vineyard, and he went to look for fruit on it but did not find any. So he said to the man who took care of the vineyard, "For three years now I've been coming to look for fruit on this fig-tree and haven't found any. Cut it down! Why should it use up the soil?"

'"Sir," the man replied, "leave it alone for one more year, and I'll dig round it and fertilise it. If it bears fruit next year, fine! If not, then cut it down."' (13.6-9)

Similarly, in the parable of the ten minas, Luke's version seems to be aimed at Israel itself and its rejection of Jesus in a way that Matthew's is not. As Matthew relates it, the man who hands out the money is simply embarking on a journey, while in Luke's he is specifically going to receive a throne. After his subjects, who hate him, send a delegation after him to say, 'We don't want this man to be our king' (19.14), he replies:

'bring them here and kill them in front of me.' (Luke 19.27)

This causes the parable's main punchline immediately beforehand to target the Jewish nation far more directly than Matthew's version:

'I tell you that to everyone who has, more will be given, but as for the one who has nothing, *even what they have will be taken away.*' (v. 26)

Luke also handles Jesus' description of the narrow and wide gates in quite a different way from the one in Matthew's Gospel. While Matthew follows up with warnings directed at any would-be believer (Matt. 7.22), Luke shows Jesus singling out his immediate Jewish audience, pointing out that their 'special privileges' might in the end prove worthless:

'Then you will say, "*We ate and drank with you, and you taught in our streets.*"

'But he will reply, "*I don't know you or where you come from. Away from me, all you evildoers!*"' (Luke 13.26-27)

He then goes on to warn his listeners that 'you yourselves' will be 'thrown out' of the kingdom of God, resulting in a great reversal in the accepted plan and order of salvation:

'... there are those who are last who will be first, and first who will be last.' (Luke 13.30)

The familiar parables of the Good Samaritan and the Prodigal Son, both unique to Luke's Gospel, also turn traditional expectations upside-down. In the first the Jews (as represented by their religious elite) fail to satisfy God's will because of their legal scruples, while the hated Samaritan does so; in the second the disobedient younger son captures the father's heart in a way that his law-abiding older brother does not. In both cases it is the least likely candidate who, surprisingly, takes centre stage.

While there is no specific reference to Jews versus Gentiles in these two stories, they do suggest that God's favour extends far beyond what established religious principles might allow. Tom Wright, comparing the homecoming of the prodigal son to Luke's later description of the admission of Gentiles into the church, writes that:

In both, people are being welcomed in from beyond the boundaries of normal acceptability. In both, this provokes grumbles from the guardians of the ancestral traditions.[1]

If Luke is showing a new direction in God's purposes in his gospel, this only seems to accelerate in the book's companion-volume, the Acts of the Apostles. Here the focus seems to wander steadily away from Israel's long-cherished hopes towards other nations and peoples. This is striking from the very outset: when the disciples ask Jesus about restoring the physical kingdom to Israel, Luke appears to show him brushing aside the question almost as unworthy of a direct answer (Acts 1.6-8).

On several occasions in Acts the blame for the crucifixion seems to be pinned squarely on the Jews, suggesting a gulf of separation opening up between believers in Jesus and the Jewish community as a whole. For instance, Peter declares to the crowd in Jerusalem on the Day of Pentecost:

*You* handed him over to be killed, and *you* disowned him before Pilate, though he had decided to let him go. *You* disowned the Holy and Righteous One and asked that a murderer be released to you. *You* killed the author of life, but God raised him from the dead. *We* are witnesses of this. (Acts 3.13-15)

This increasing sense of 'us' and 'them' seems to be underlined by Stephen, the first Christian martyr, who is even more scathing when he addresses the Sanhedrin:

'You stiff-necked people! Your hearts and ears are still uncircumcised. You are just like your ancestors: you always resist the Holy Spirit! Was there ever a prophet your ancestors did not persecute? They even killed those who predicted the coming of the Righteous One. And now you have betrayed and murdered him – you who have received the law that was given through angels but have not obeyed it.' (Acts 7.51-53)

From this point on Luke takes us on a journey. A series of events shows God apparently shifting the goalposts to extend the offer of salvation beyond the confines of Judaism itself. The pace is such that even those early Jewish believers in Jesus are taken by surprise: Peter, the leader of the mission to the Jews, has to be shown the same vision three times, and then have messengers sent to him, before he is willing to visit the house of a Gentile.

What happens when he reaches the house of Cornelius astonishes him even more. While he is preaching, God pours out his Spirit out spontaneously on an uncircumcised Gentile audience. Ultimately he is prompted to make a statement, utterly extraordinary for a Jew, that the Old Testament law was 'a yoke that neither we nor our ancestors have been able to bear' and that 'we believe it is through the grace of our Lord Jesus that we are saved, just as they [Gentile believers] are' (Acts 15.10-11).

The dramatic shift of attention away from the Jewish mission to the Gentiles becomes more apparent in the preaching of Paul, as Luke records it. Over and over again, while the Jews reject the gospel, the Gentiles welcome it with open arms. The passage placed at the end of the book, describing Paul's encounter with leading figures of the Jewish community in Rome, sums this up rather well:

They disagreed among themselves and began to leave after Paul had made this final statement: 'The Holy Spirit spoke the truth to your ancestors when he said through Isaiah the prophet:

'"Go to this people and say,
'You will be ever hearing but never understanding;
   you will be ever seeing but never perceiving.'
For this people's heart has become calloused;
   they hardly hear with their ears,
   and they have closed their eyes.
Otherwise they might see with their eyes,
   hear with their ears,
   understand with their hearts
and turn, and I would heal them."

'Therefore I want you to know that *God's salvation has been sent to the Gentiles*, and they will listen!' (Acts 28.25-28)

What is Luke trying to tell us here? Have the Jews lost their status before God? Does the steady shift in the focus of the book from Jerusalem to Rome imply a permanent switch of God's s favour from one people to another?

In order to answer this question, we need to go back to the very beginning of Luke's gospel. What are the clues as to his ultimate intentions in writing? How does he see Jews and Gentiles within the overall purposes of God?

Firstly we should note that Luke's Jesus is just as much the Jewish Messiah that he is in Matthew. In the first two chapters Luke underlines Jesus' Jewish pedigree as vividly as Matthew does, and deliberately imitates the style of the Septuagint, the Greek translation of the Jewish scriptures, to evoke the atmosphere of the Old Testament.

In fact, if Matthew bases his picture of Jesus on Moses, Luke's model may be partly drawn from Samuel, whose miraculous conception arouses a strikingly similar response to that of Mary (1 Sam 2.1-10; Luke 1.46-55), who grew 'in stature and in favour with the LORD and with people' (1 Sam 2.26, cf. Luke 2.52) and whose exposure of a corrupt priesthood leads to the glory departing from Israel (1 Sam 3.18; 4.22; cf. Luke 13.34-35).

This reference back to a great leader from Israel's past is surely no coincidence. In Chapter 1 it is the angel Gabriel, previously introduced in scripture announcing the news of the coming Messiah to Daniel (Dan. 9.20-27), who tells Mary that Jesus is coming specifically to reign as king over the Jewish people, not just at some vague time in the future, but for all eternity:

'The Lord God will give him the throne of his father David, and *he will reign over Jacob's descendants for ever*; his kingdom will never end.' (Luke 1.32-33)

Later Mary herself reaffirms God's promises of blessing made to Abraham and his offspring:

'He has helped his servant Israel,
  remembering to be merciful
*to Abraham and his descendants for ever*,
  just as he promised our ancestors.' (1.54-55)

Similarly Zechariah, the father of John the Baptist, sees the coming Saviour fulfilling traditional Jewish expectations of the Messiah and his rule:

'He has raised up a horn of salvation for us
  in the house of his servant David
(as he said through his holy prophets of long ago),
salvation from our enemies
  and from the hand of all who hate us –
to show mercy to our ancestors
  and *to remember his holy covenant,
  the oath he swore to our father Abraham*.' (Luke 1.69-73)

The prophetess Anna, too, seems to recognise Jesus as Messiah in conventional Jewish terms, as she 'spoke about the child to all who were looking forward to the redemption of Jerusalem' (2.38).

Significantly, Luke says nothing to undermine such viewpoints: for him, the Jews still appear to be the people of God (1.77; 2.32), and the coming of Jesus marks simply a new stage in Israel's history, the fulfilment of everything that has gone before. We read, for example, how Mary and Joseph scrupulously fulfilled the requirements of the Old Testament law (2.39), brought their son up to attend and participate in Jewish festivals on a regular basis (2.41), and how Jesus himself developed an insatiable appetite for the Old Testament scriptures (2.46) and a love for the temple in Jerusalem (2.49).

Against such a background, the judgement of the nation implied later in the parables of the unfruitful fig tree or the ten minas represents nothing new. Such warnings appear frequently throughout the Old Testament, within the framework of God's unshakeable promises to Israel. But, as the Old Testament continually reminds us, such judgements, however harsh, never imply that God has permanently abandoned his people.

Even when Luke presents Jesus' teaching on the wide and narrow doors, with his more pointed warnings of total rejection, the message is firmly aimed at individuals. The dangers of complacency that can come from a sense of a special standing with God are equally ones which should be heeded by Christians today.

Nor can the parables of the Good Samaritan or the Prodigal Son be said to be criticising Jews as such. Even if we stretched the second story in this way, given that the older son is seeking, mistakenly, to 'earn' his father's favour through works of obedience, it would be a futile defence for replacement theology, since the father emphatically tells him,

'My son ... you are always with me, and *everything I have is yours*.' (15.31)

In fact, as the first two verses of chapter 15 clearly show, Jesus is once more contrasting those on the margins of Judaism - such as the Pharisees and the tax collectors - with those on the 'inside'.

Elsewhere we see the same pattern. In Luke 16.19-31 it is the poor beggar who goes to Abraham's bosom - not the rich man. In Luke 18.9-14 it is the tax-collector who goes home in a right relationship with God - not the Pharisee. In these and other stories, *all* those involved are Jews: but it is the complacent and self-righteous who are heading for judgement. While Jesus may have come to cause 'the falling and rising of many in Israel' (Luke 2.34), this was in no sense an outright rejection of the Jewish people as a whole.

So what of Acts? Firstly, Jesus in no way throws out of court his disciples' question about the restoration of the kingdom to Israel in Acts 1.6-8. He has already hinted at such a restoration in Luke 21.24 and 22.30 (as does Peter in Acts 3.21), and it is simply the timing he refuses to discuss. In fact, if Jesus had believed that God would permanently abandon Israel as a specially chosen nation, *this would have been the ideal moment to say so*. Conspicuously, he makes no such remark.

Nor is it clear that Acts pins the blame for Jesus' death on the Jews. Luke has already reported Jesus warning that it would be *the Gentiles* who would 'flog him and kill him' (Luke 18.32-33). Although Peter holds his 'fellow Jews' (2.14) accountable for what has taken place (2.23), he later joins in a prayer which recognises that others are to blame and only mentions the Jews *last,* before finally concluding that it is *the Father himself* who was the prime mover:

'Indeed Herod and Pontius Pilate met together with the Gentiles and the people of Israel in this city to conspire against your holy servant Jesus, whom you anointed. They did what *your power and will had decided beforehand* should happen.'

(Acts 4.27-28)[2]

Significantly, Luke has already quoted Jesus on the cross as praying, *'Father, forgive them, for they do not know what they are doing'* (Luke 23.34). These words clearly recall the last verse of Isaiah 53 ('For he bore the sin of many, and made intercession for the transgressors'), which, earlier in the chapter, makes very much the same point:

Yet *it was the LORD's will* to crush him and cause him to suffer

(Is. 53.10)

Neither does Acts show the early church breaking free from its Jewish roots. Far from depicting an entirely new religion, Luke's portrait of the church shows remarkable similarities with other sects *within* Judaism at the time, most particularly the Essenes (the probable authors of the Dead Sea Scrolls). Like them, he shows the early Jewish Christians pooling their resources, eating together and treating the religious authorities with great suspicion. And there are other similarities between the two groups: they both shared the belief that marriage was restricted to one husband and one wife (this did not become universal among Jews until much later), that taking oaths was wrong in principle, that lying about property was an offence of the utmost seriousness, and that a specially appointed person should administer a common purse.[3]

However, it is also striking to see how, unlike the Essenes, Luke records the early church recognising the ongoing significance of the temple. They continued to meet in public to worship together in the temple courts. And the Jewish origin of the gospel remains clear even when the good news is first shared with the Gentiles: for Peter, the gospel he is sharing is 'the message God sent *to the people of Israel*' (Acts 10.36). For Paul, talking to a Jewish audience, Jesus remains the 'hope of Israel' (Acts 28.20).

Nor is Luke's view of the Jewish law wholly negative. The Council of Jerusalem that he describes in Acts 15 did not abandon the Law but waived almost all of it for Gentiles. The compromise reached falls short of Paul's ideal but achieves harmony within the church. Paul, he tells us, has Timothy circumcised to avoid causing needless offence in Acts 16.3, and observes a Jewish purification rite in Acts 21.24. Ananias, who first laid hands on Saul, is described as 'a devout observer of the law' (Acts 22.12). And Luke paints a more favourable picture of the law-abiding Pharisees than some other gospel writers (Luke 13.31; Acts 5.34-39; 23.6, 9; 26.5).

Finally, Luke does not give the impression that by switching the focus to the Gentiles, the gospel is waning among the Jews. Where Acts 21.20 refers to 'many thousands' of Jews who have become believers in Jesus, the Greek word would be better translated 'myriads': 'tens of thousands' (CEV); 'thousands upon thousands' (Message). Indeed, Luke is scrupulously even-handed in his portrayal of Peter, as apostle to the Jews, and Paul, as apostle to the Gentiles. Both receive significant visions; both receive unwelcome veneration, both raise the dead, both experience miraculous prison escapes, and both heal through unusual means (Peter's shadow and Paul's handkerchief).

What, then, is Luke's view of God's purposes for the Jewish people? A clue to the answer may lie in two significant stories at the beginning and end of his gospel. In both cases God withholds something in response to unbelief but restores it finally in a dramatic moment of recognition. The first case is that of Zechariah, who is struck dumb when he disbelieves the angel's message, but whose tongue is loosed when, against family precedent, he declares that his son's name will be John (1.63-64).

The second example is that of Cleopas and another disciple, who completely without realising are talking to the risen Jesus on the road to Emmaus after the crucifixion. He reproves them for their unbelief (24.16, 25), and yet 'their eyes were kept from recognizing him'. Only after they press him to come in and eat with them are their eyes opened, and they fully grasp the truth for themselves.

In the context of both the gospel and Acts, these accounts share a rich symbolism. For Luke, as for the other gospel writers, physical impairment is a picture of spiritual impairment, and physical blindness a picture of spiritual blindness. Yet such disability need not be permanent. For instance, in Luke 19.42, Jesus cries over Jerusalem,

'If you, even you, had only known on this day what would bring you peace – but now it is *hidden from your eyes.*'

Yet earlier in the gospel he hints that this state of blindness will one day change:

'you will not see me again *until you say*, "Blessed is he who comes in the name of the Lord."' (13.35)

The same theme of temporary spiritual blindness remains important through Acts. In two striking cases, that of Paul and of the sorcerer Elymas, God counters opposition to the Christian message by causing short-term physical blindness, resulting ultimately in the gospel bearing fruit among the Gentiles (Acts 9.8-18; 13.6-12). This leap from blindness to sight ties in with Paul's own commission to both Jew and Gentile 'to *open their eyes* and turn them from darkness to light, and from the power of Satan to God' (26.18).

This may give added significance to the verses from Isaiah 6 which Paul quotes at the end of Acts, when the bulk of the Jews in Rome reject his message:

'For this people's heart has become calloused; they hardly hear with their ears, and *they have closed their eyes*. Otherwise they might see with their eyes, hear with their ears, understand with their hearts and turn, and I would heal them.' (Acts 28.27)

What can we conclude from this? In the two previous cases in Acts God himself causes a blindness to come so that the gospel can be preached to the Gentiles - *but the blindness was only short-lived!* Could it be, therefore, as with the Zechariah and Cleopas stories, that Luke is suggesting a similar situation at the end of Acts, in relation to the Jewish people themselves?

If this is true, we may find here echoes of Paul's earlier remark about Israel in his letter to the Romans, paraphrasing Deuteronomy 29.4,

'God gave them a spirit of stupor,
  *eyes that could not see*
  and ears that could not hear,
to this very day.' (Rom. 11.8)

Yet Paul is able to conclude with the triumphant affirmation:

I do not want you to be ignorant of this mystery, brothers and sisters, so that you may not be conceited: Israel has experienced a hardening in part *until* the full number of the Gentiles has come in, and in this way all Israel will be saved. (Rom. 11.25-26)

If Luke's thinking parallels Paul's thinking at this point, then the last chapter of Acts has yet to be written. The Emmaus story provides a key for the whole of Luke's account. Temporarily unable to see what ought to be obvious, and only understanding Jesus as a 'prophet' (Luke 24.19) the Jews will one day join Cleopas and his companion on the road to Emmaus in their climactic moment of revelation and recognise him as their long-awaited Messiah.

# 7 RECONSIDERING JOHN

So far we have established that the gospels of Matthew and Luke fall well short of proving a case for 'replacement theology'. In both cases the story of Jesus is woven into the background of first century Judaism in its various intricate strands, and while he vigorously challenges the practices of some groups within that mix, he never rejects his Jewish heritage outright.

But what about the gospel of John? Here the atmosphere is quite different: the contrasts are sharper, and the conflicts more pointed. The details of Jesus' Jewish ancestry and upbringing seem obscured: he appears as if from nowhere and seems at one remove from his ethnic background. While both Matthew and Luke begin by presenting Jesus as the climax of Jewish hopes for the Messiah, John reveals him to be the ultimate representation of God himself, untainted by national or tribal boundaries.

This sense of a radical shift becomes clearer as the gospel progresses. John's language brings out a clear separation between the followers of Jesus and the rest of the population: when Pilate asks Jesus whether he is 'King of the Jews', he replies that 'my kingdom is not of this world' (John 18.36) and earlier in the same verse distinguishes 'my servants', his disciples, from 'the Jews', as if his followers were somehow no longer Jewish themselves.

Indeed, throughout the gospel, John appears to use the label 'the Jews' in a negative sense for Jesus' religious opponents. At one point, in a series of highly-charged exchanges, he seems to describe them as children of the devil (8.44). The same hint appears in Revelation (which, though now almost universally regarded by scholars as the work of a different author, shares much of the gospel's imagery and number symbolism). Here we find two references to a 'synagogue of Satan' (2.9; 3.9). The natural impression on reading such passages might well be that the Jews have forfeited any continuing right to be considered as God's people.

Another way in which Jesus appears to distance himself from the Judaism of his time is in telling his listeners that they are 'not my sheep' (10.26). Since in this passage he is presenting himself as 'the good shepherd' who is consciously taking on the role of Yahweh, the 'Shepherd of Israel' in the Old Testament, it could be easily argued that he is attempting to establish a new Israel, now universal in scope, in which the Jews no longer have a decisive role.

This might also be seen in the way that John reinterprets passages which in the Old Testament applied purely to Israel, to give them a universal significance. For instance, where Zechariah 12.10, the great promise of Jewish national repentance, says that 'the house of David and the inhabitants of Jerusalem' will 'look on me, the one they have pierced', we find John seeing the Roman soldiers at the cross as fulfilling it (John 19.34-37). A further widening of the same verse takes place in Revelation 1.7, where 'all peoples on earth' will now be gazing and mourning when Jesus returns, suggesting a complete realignment of the original promise.

This novel attitude towards the Old Testament is apparent in other aspects as well. For example, instead of affirming the ten commandments as he does in the other gospels, Jesus offers what he describes as a new commandment to his disciples (John 13.34, 15.12-17; compare 1 John 4.21). And on several occasions he seems to dismiss passages from the Old Testament as 'your law' or 'their law', almost as if it were nothing to do with him.

The first of Jesus' miracles, at Cana in Galilee, seems to confirm this break with tradition. Here he takes water set aside for traditional Jewish purification rites and turns it into wine. The story seems to portray the replacement of an old order with something new and better: the established method of cleansing has become redundant.

Perhaps the strongest evidence for a fundamental shift in God's purposes, however, appears in chapter 4 of the gospel. Jesus is here talking to a Samaritan woman who raises a common bone of contention between Samaritans and Jews:

'Our ancestors worshipped on this mountain, but you Jews claim that the place where we must worship is in Jerusalem.' (v. 20)

Jesus' reply is very instructive. He says,

'Woman, … a time is coming when you will worship the Father neither on this mountain nor in Jerusalem. … Yet a time is coming and has now come when the true worshippers will worship the Father in the Spirit and in truth, for they are the kind of worshippers the Father seeks'. (vv.21-23)

It seems natural to conclude here that Jesus has moved a large step ahead from the outlook of first century Judaism. True worship will no longer be about special places, special times, special seasons, special foods, special people. Through the death, resurrection and ascension of the Messiah, the focus of true faith is switching from the particular to the universal, from the physical to the spiritual, from the visible to the invisible realms. Now that we can worship the Father in the Spirit and in truth, the core practices of Old Testament Judaism are a mere shadow of a greater reality.

So does John's Jesus really see himself as Jewish at all? Is he turning his back on his Jewish heritage? Or does he think of himself as establishing a new Israel? And how much of this is John's own interpretation?

The first problem to address is John's strange use of the expression 'the Jews'. The difficulty for us is that the people that John calls 'Jews' appear to be set in a different category from others who are obviously Jewish as well. These supposed 'non-Jews' include John the Baptist and his followers (1.19; 3.25), as well as Jesus (2.18-20 etc.) and the disciples (11.8, 13.33). Most extraordinary of all, they even include Joseph of Arimathea, who was a member of the Jewish ruling council (19.38)!

This apparent distinction also applies to the people that Jesus healed, even though they and their families were all clearly Jewish themselves, as the following example shows:

The **Jews** did not believe that he had been blind and had received his sight, until they called the parents of the man who had received his sight ... (His parents said these things because they feared the **Jews**, for the **Jews** had already agreed that if anyone should confess Jesus to be Christ, he was to be put out of the synagogue.) (9.18, 22 ESV)

More puzzling still is the way that, at one point, 'the Jews' are contrasted with 'the people', ignoring the fact that *both* groups are clearly Jewish:

**The Jews** were looking for him at the feast, and saying, "Where is he?" And there was much muttering about him among **the people**. While some said, "He is a good man", others said, "No, he is leading the people astray." Yet for fear of **the Jews** no one spoke openly of him. (7.11-13 ESV)

Despite this, Jesus is clearly acknowledged to be Jewish, by John himself (1.11), by his disciple Nathanael (1.49), by the unnamed Samaritan woman (4.9) and by Pilate himself

(18.35). Moreover, Jesus affirms this own Jewishness in the clearest of terms:

You Samaritans worship what you do not know; *we worship what we do know,* for *salvation is from the Jews.* (4.22)

How do we account for these glaring discrepancies? It becomes clear on closer inspection that John is using the term in different ways depending on the context. A number of these are purely neutral, such as 'a feast of the Jews' (5.1 ESV). And on at least one occasion, the word seems to imply 'Judeans' as opposed to 'Galileans':

After this Jesus went about in Galilee. He would not go about in Judea, because the **Jews** [Judeans] were seeking to kill him.
(7.1 ESV)

On the vast majority of occasions, however, John seems to use 'the Jews' as a shorthand for 'Jewish leaders' (which is how the NIV usually translates the expression). Why he should do this is open to debate.[1] While it may seem strange that he uses 'Jews' to exclude the vast majority of the Jewish population, we should note that Josephus, the greatest Jewish writer of his time, does the same in his *Jewish Wars,* where he frequently uses the term in a restrictive sense to describe the Zealots defending Jerusalem.[2]

While such shorthand might seem puzzling, it is worth recognising that we often do the same in modern English. If someone talks about the Americans invading Iraq in 2003, they certainly do not mean the entire population of North and South America, or even every person in the United

States. What they really mean is a contingent of the US army and air force at the behest of the President and Congress (and with a considerable body of opposition at home).

In fact, such language is by no means unique in the Bible. Anyone reading Joshua chapter 13, verse 12, would be forgiven for thinking that Moses had conquered he entire kingdom of Og in Bashan single-handedly! Similarly, earlier in the same book, we find the expression 'all Israel' clearly not implying 'all Israel':

Then Joshua, together with **all Israel**, took Achan son of Zerah, the silver, the robe, the gold bar, his sons and daughters, his cattle, donkeys and sheep, his tent and all that he had, to the Valley of Achor. … Then **all Israel** stoned him, and after they had stoned the rest, they burned them. (Josh. 7.24-25)

(Given that the population of Israel ran into hundreds of thousands, a literal fulfilment of this passage would have been very difficult!)

Another parallel appears elsewhere in John's gospel, where John himself explains on one occasion that when he uses the word 'Jesus' he is actually referring to others:

Now Jesus learned that the Pharisees had heard that *he was gaining and baptising more disciples* than John – although in fact *it was not Jesus who baptised, but his disciples.* (4.1-2)

We are, then, clearly touching the deep connection between the 'one' and 'the many' that runs through much of the Old Testament and clearly spills into the New. We noted this in Chapter Three where we saw how in Isaiah 'the servant of the LORD' refers both to Israel as a whole, and to a servant *within* Israel. It does remind us of the need to understand words as their authors originally intended them, rather than placing our own preconceptions on what they might actually mean.

What, then, of the extremely confrontational language of the gospel? It seems that John is highlighting the sense of 'us' and 'them' in some of the exchanges to develop one of his main themes: the contrast between belief and unbelief, light and darkness. Here it is striking that the same kind of 'distancing' language that Jesus uses towards 'the Jews', he directs even at members of his own family:

Therefore Jesus told them, 'My time is not yet here; for you any time will do. The world cannot hate you, but it hates me because I testify that its works are evil. (7.6-7)

However, to imply that John's Gospel is somehow unique when talking this way is very wide of the mark. The conflict between the followers of Shammai and Hillel, two leading teachers from the previous century, is well-documented: in one regrettable incident shortly before the Fall of Jerusalem, some leading Hillelites were trapped in a house and murdered when they refused to give their support to the insurgency against the Romans.

Similarly, Jesus' description of his listeners as children of the devil is not entirely one-way: he is accused in other gospels of casting demons out by Beelzebub, while in John he is accused of being possessed by a demon himself (John

8.48, 52), and the Talmud later charges him with sorcery and attempting to lead Israel astray.[3]

In fact, the accusation that John is being anti-Semitic in including such remarks completely ignores the wider context of the New Testament. In Matthew 13.38 we find 'sons of the kingdom' contrasted with the 'sons of the evil one' (ESV), while Jesus later accuses the religious leaders in Matthew as being 'children of hell' and a 'brood of vipers' (23.15, 33), an expression which John the Baptist also uses (3.7). And Yahweh is no less severe in the Old Testament, accusing Israel of adultery, prostitution, idolatry and murder. The language is strong and confrontational because of the gravity of what is at stake.

But it is not just Jews who are seen in these terms. In his first letter, John defines 'the children of the devil' by their actions and attitudes, not by their racial origins (1 John 3.10). Indeed, the New Testament sees anyone who has not been reconciled to God through Christ as being under the devil's control: in Ephesians Paul reminds his Gentile readers how they originally 'followed the ways of this world and of *the ruler of the kingdom of the air*, the spirit who is now at work in those who are disobedient' (2.2) and then goes on to say that '*all of us* [Jew *and* Gentile] also lived among them at one time' (v. 3). Similarly he writes to the Corinthians that '*the god of this age* has blinded the minds of unbelievers, so that they cannot see the light of the gospel that displays the glory of Christ' (2 Cor 4.4). And he recounts that his initial commission from Christ was to open the eyes of 'your own people' and 'the

Gentiles', to 'turn them from darkness to light, and *from the power of Satan to God*' (Acts 26.17-18).

In this sense, we are probably asking the wrong question, and missing the point of what Jesus is saying when he accuses his listeners of being controlled by the devil. The thrust of his warning can be applied to anyone, whether they regard themselves as 'Jewish' or 'Christian', who regard salvation as an automatic right because of family descent, obedience to rules, church or synagogue attendance, christening, circumcision or any such outward mark, short of a personal relationship and daily walk with Jesus Christ.

When Jesus uses strong language such as this, it is to reflect the utmost seriousness of the situation of those who feel they have no need of God's redemption, not to demonise those he came to die for. If he could call his own disciples 'evil' (compare Matt. 5.1-2 with 7.11) and say even to his closest friend, 'Get behind me, Satan!' (Matt. 16.23), we should hardly be surprised. While the world of today may be painted in fifty shades of grey, everything that Jesus says is in stark black and white. There is no escaping from it: if we are not for him, we are against him.

The same can be said about some of the strongly-worded expressions in Revelation. For Christians reading the book at a time of intense persecution, the various references to Satan's activities throughout Revelation would naturally have suggested the emperor worship that was being enforced by the Roman authorities on pain of death. The mention of Satan's 'throne' in Pergamum, for example, almost certainly describes one of the oldest temples devoted to emperor worship in Asia Minor.

The two references in Revelation to a 'synagogue of Satan', therefore, explained as those 'who claim to be Jews though they are not' (3.9), make perfect sense in relation to this. A second century inscription found in Smyrna,[4] one of the two cities mentioned with a 'synagogue of Satan', uses the words *hoi pote Ioudaioi*, (meaning 'people who were formerly Jews'), probably suggesting those who had abandoned or compromised their Jewishness.[5] Although Judaism was an officially protected religion, and therefore Jews were not under the same intense pressure as Christians to burn incense to the emperor, it is entirely possible that the 'synagogue of Satan' refers to those Jews who had sold out to the Roman authorities out of a desire to conform and win prestige.

What, then, are we to say about the apparently disparaging references to 'your law'? Do these not suggest that Jesus was distancing himself from the entire Old Testament?

Firstly, we should note that at various points in the gospel (5.39, 7.19 and 7.23) Jesus presents a very positive view of the Old Testament. Indeed, after one of the 'your law' verses, he goes on to declare that 'Scripture cannot be set aside' (John 10.35). He himself keeps the Father's commandments to 'remain in his love' (15.10). He regularly attended Jewish feasts and celebrations (Passover - 2.13; an unnamed feast - 5.1; Tabernacles - 7.10): and even one (the Feast of Dedication, or Hanukkah) not enjoined by the Old Testament itself (10.22).[6] This hardly sounds like he is divorcing himself from the heritage and practices of Judaism.

Secondly, we find similar turns of phrase elsewhere in the Bible. In Matthew, Jesus asks the Pharisees and teachers of the law 'why do you break the command of God for the sake of *your tradition*?' (15.3). He later describes the forefathers of Israel as '*your ancestors*' (23.32), as does Stephen in Acts 7.51. And in the Old Testament, Yahweh frequently appears to distance himself from Israel in a similar manner, as in the following example:

Then the LORD said to Moses, 'Go down, because *your people*, whom you brought up out of Egypt, have become corrupt.

(Ex. 32.7)

Thirdly, John is keen, like Matthew, to show that Jesus is the *fulfilment* of the Old Testament, with all scripture pointing to him (5.39). This is apparent not only in the titles he gives to Jesus, such as 'Lamb of God'; 'King of Israel', 'Bread of Life', 'True Vine'; but also by using a formula similar to Matthew's favourite 'this was to fulfil ...' in 19.36.

Strangely enough, one of the 'your law' verses we are considering here is actually another classic example of this:

But *this is to fulfil* what is written in *their Law*: "They hated me without reason." (15.25)

However, the key point in each of the passages in question is that Jesus has just talked about his unity with the Father (8.16-18; 10.28-34; 15.23-25). In other words, Jesus can look at scripture from one remove because in each case he is talking as Yahweh in person: the one who gave the Old Testament law but who also transcends it. He is *himself* the Word of God (John 1.1), the true embodiment of what without him is just a shadow. It is this context that he can, as in Matthew 5, lay down *new* commandments which fulfil and clarify what has gone before. It is not that Jesus has come to *replace* the Old Testament; he comes instead, as we have already said, to *complete* it.

In this context, we should ask what Jesus meant when he was saying to the Samaritan woman that 'God is spirit'. Clearly he was directing her away from the question of *the place* where God should be worshipped. But was he implying a rejection of all special times, places, days, seasons, people, objects or actions that are rooted in the physical world, as an outdated relic of a bygone age?

If we believe this, we ought to consider the implications of such an idea very carefully. If this were *completely* true we would all have dispensed with baptism, communion, anointing oil, pastors and elders, Sunday worship, the laying on of hands, Christmas, Easter, Pentecost and so on. The list could be endless. The continuing existence of such sacred rites, objects and times in the church remains for us, as before, outward pointers to an invisible reality.

The danger here is that a non-Biblical Greek worldview, with its inherent suspicion of the material world, is being substituted for a Biblical, Jewish one. Rather as Jesus *summarises* rather than *abolishes* the Law, so he *simplifies* rather than *abolishes* the physical symbols of a heavenly reality.

The ongoing existence of such practices within the church suggests that God still mediates in physical ways: Paul used a handkerchief, Jesus spat, the apostles laid hands, Peter's shadow fell, the woman touched the hem of Jesus' garment.

Of course, we could manage without any of these, since we live by faith and not by sight - but God in his sovereign mercy has chosen for the supernatural world to *intersect* with the physical one. This is the whole point of the (invisible) Word becoming (visible) flesh, and to deny it is to deny the very purpose of the incarnation itself.

Rather than *abolishing* the physical nature of our existence, the incarnation *raises it to a higher level*: there is now a *human being* (and a Jew at that!) at the right hand of God, still bearing the marks of his wounds at Calvary, forever interceding for us. With the ascension of Jesus, God has not *withdrawn* from the physical realm, but has *embraced* it in a more powerful way to secure its entire redemption (Eph. 1.10).

In conclusion, therefore, John does not teach a theology of replacement, but of enrichment. He shows that God's plan of salvation is truly universal in scope, with Israel as the first step in his purposes for the whole of humankind. With the coming of Jesus, the covenant promises to Israel are to be enlarged to include Gentiles as well:

I have other sheep that are not of this sheepfold. I must bring them also. They too will listen to my voice, and there shall be *one* flock and *one* shepherd. (John 10.16)

The same idea emerges when John quotes the High Priest as prophesying (without realising the full significance of his words) that Jesus would die '*not only* for [the Jewish] nation *but also* for the scattered children of God, to bring them together and make them *one*.' (11.52).

As we noted in Chapter One, because the first of these statements is followed so soon afterwards by the declaration that 'I and the Father are *one*', it seems natural to assume that in Chapter 17, when Jesus prays that *we* should be *one* as *he and the Father* are *one* (v. 22), he is echoing the imagery of 'one flock and one shepherd' where the 'us' should be a church composed Jews and Gentiles together (John 10.16).

While this may appear a giant leap forward from the remit of the Old Testament, the thrust of John's gospel is simply building on what has gone before. The Jewish people, though many rejected him, are still 'his own' (1.11). He remains the Jewish Messiah (1.41), the King of Israel (1.49), the King of the Jews (18.33).

This continuity is also apparent in Revelation: Jesus is worshipped in heaven as 'the Lion of the tribe of Judah' (5.5), the central significance of Jerusalem is affirmed (11.2, 21.2) and a faithful Jewish remnant is preserved (7.5-8) alongside those 'from every nation, tribe, people and language' (7.9). As we saw in Chapter Four, the preservation of the woman in the wilderness in 12.6 (a clear picture of the scattered nation of Israel) *after* the Messiah's first coming reveals God's ongoing purposes for the Jewish people, who are shown to be *distinct* from the followers of Jesus (12.17), while the symbolism of twenty-four elders in 4.4 and 11.16 seems to depict the twelve sons of Jacob *and* the twelve apostles together: a picture, perhaps, of Israel and the church *alongside* each other (compare 21.12-14).

If this were not enough, we can hardly miss the significance of the last few verses of the book: Jesus is coming back not as a disembodied spirit, nor in the guise of a Gentile ruler, but as 'the Root and the Offspring of David' (22.16).

There could be no clearer affirmation of the Old Testament hope. Scripture concludes with a ringing endorsement of a *Jewish* Messiah, exalted in the heavens, who will one day return to claim his inheritance and establish his rule on earth. One day the whole world will bow down in awe and, in witnessing the glory of Jesus, will recognize with total astonishment that 'salvation is from the Jews' (John 4.22).

# 8 RECONSIDERING PAUL

Much of what we have read in the last three chapters involves an element of guesswork in exploring the outlook of the gospel writers. Save for a few scant details elsewhere in the New Testament, we know very little about the authors themselves or their mindset outside the writings they left us.

With Paul, however, the situation is completely different. Because of the extensive information that is provided for us both in Acts and from his own letters, we know a great deal about his life, his motivations and his inner conflicts. It is Paul who is often seen as playing the crucial role in redefining the relationship between Judaism and the church. It is he who often gets the blame or the credit, according to one's viewpoint, for selling the faith he grew up in down the river, or for liberating Christianity from the shackles of an increasingly legalistic brand of Judaism.

Certainly a strong case could be made for seeing Paul as a trailblazer for 'replacement theology'. Having been brought up as a Pharisee, and trained under Gamaliel, one of the most celebrated and enlightened Jewish teachers of his age, he became one of the sternest critics of Pharisaic Judaism after his dramatic vision of Christ on the Damascus Road.

His letters show much about how this experience of the risen Lord Jesus completely altered his outlook. To begin with, he appears completely to redefine what it means to be a Jew:

A person is not a Jew who is one only outwardly, nor is circumcision merely outward and physical. No, a person is a Jew who is one inwardly; and circumcision is circumcision of the heart, by the Spirit, not by the written code. (Rom. 2.28-29)

Because this relies on an inward work, rather than an outward mark or physical descent, he saw that anyone could attain to this privileged status through God's sovereign choice and calling:

For not all who are descended from Israel are Israel. Nor because they are his descendants are they all Abraham's children. On the contrary, 'It is through Isaac that your offspring will be reckoned.' In other words, it is not the children by physical descent who are God's children, but it is the children of the promise who are regarded as Abraham's offspring. (Rom. 9.6-8)

Consequently, it is our response of faith to that choice, and that alone, which enables us to receive the blessings given to Abraham and his descendants, which are now no longer restricted to the Jewish people alone:

Understand, then, that those who have faith are children of Abraham. Scripture foresaw that God would justify the Gentiles by faith, and announced the gospel in advance to Abraham: 'All nations will be blessed through you.' So those who rely on faith are blessed along with Abraham, the man of faith. ... So in Christ Jesus you are all children of God through faith.

(Gal. 3.7-9, 26)

In this sense the people of God in the Old Testament have now become our own direct forerunners in the faith. For instance, Paul is able to write to the Greek inhabitants of Corinth:

For I do not want you to be ignorant of the fact, brothers and sisters, that *our ancestors* were all under the cloud and that they all passed through the sea. (1 Cor. 10.1)

From this many would argue that for Paul, the church is now the true Israel in God's sight:

Neither circumcision nor uncircumcision means anything; what counts is the new creation. Peace and mercy to all who follow this rule – to the *Israel of God.* (Gal. 6.15-16)

Watch out for those dogs, those evildoers, those mutilators of the flesh. For it is *we* who are the circumcision, *we* who serve God by his Spirit ... (Phil. 3.2-3)

So great is this realignment that Paul can now, in a letter primarily addressed to non-Jewish converts, use the word 'Gentiles' as a term for 'non-Christians':

So I tell you this, and insist on it in the Lord, that you must no longer live as the *Gentiles* do, in the futility of their thinking.
(Eph. 4.17)

If this is the case, one could easily argue that the Jewish nation has forever lost its privileged position in God's purposes. In Christ there is no favouritism (Rom. 2.11) as all racial distinctions have been dissolved:

Here there is no Gentile or Jew, circumcised or uncircumcised, barbarian, Scythian, slave or free, but Christ is all, and is in all.
(Col. 3.11)

... for all of you who were baptised into Christ have clothed yourselves with Christ. There is neither Jew nor Gentile, neither slave nor free, nor is there male and female, for you are all one in Christ Jesus. If you belong to Christ, then you are Abraham's seed, and heirs according to the promise.       (Gal. 3.27-29)

Such a viewpoint might well suggest that natural, physical Israel has served its purpose but no longer has a valid destiny as such before God. Christ has fulfilled the law on our behalf (Rom. 8.3; 10.4) and the old covenant has been superseded. Paul writes in his letter to the Galatians:

Tell me, you who want to be under the law, are you not aware of what the law says? For it is written that Abraham had two sons, one by the slave woman and the other by the free woman. His son by the slave woman was born according to the flesh, but his son by the free woman was born as the result of a divine promise.

These things are being taken figuratively: the women represent two covenants. One covenant is from Mount Sinai and bears children who are to be slaves: this is Hagar. Now Hagar stands for Mount Sinai in Arabia and corresponds to the present city of

Jerusalem, because she is in slavery with her children. But the Jerusalem that is above is free, and she is our mother. For it is written:

'Be glad, barren woman,
   you who never bore a child;
break forth and cry aloud,
   you who were never in labour;
because more are the children of the
   desolate woman
      than of her who has a husband.'

Now you, brothers and sisters, like Isaac, are children of promise. At that time the son born according to the flesh persecuted the son born by the power of the Spirit. It is the same now. But what does Scripture say? 'Get rid of the slave woman and her son, for the slave woman's son will never share in the inheritance with the free woman's son.' Therefore, brothers and sisters, we are not children of the slave woman, but of the free woman.                                    (Gal. 4.21-31)

This is not the only passage in Paul's letters to suggest a sharp parting of the ways from the Jewish community as a whole. To the Thessalonians he writes:

For you, brothers and sisters, became imitators of God's churches in Judea, which are in Christ Jesus: you suffered from your own people the same things those churches suffered from the Jews who killed the Lord Jesus and the prophets and also drove us out. They displease God and are hostile to everyone in their effort to keep us from speaking to the Gentiles so that they may be saved. In this way they always heap up their sins to the limit. The wrath of God has come upon them at last.
                                    (1 Thess. 2.14-16)

From these passages we might gain a strong sense that God has now finished in his dealings with the Jewish nation.

The church is now the true 'Israel', and as such inherits all the blessings previously accorded to the Jews in the Old Testament, who now stand in opposition to his plans.

But is this the whole story? Missing important clues can lead to very misleading conclusions. Reading Paul's letters more thoroughly reveals a much more nuanced picture.

We began by suggesting that in chapter 2 of Romans Paul might be redefining what it means to be a Jew. However, there is nothing in the chapter which implies a *broadening* of the boundaries of Judaism. In fact, he is reaching for a *narrower* definition of what it means to be a 'Jew' rather than extending it: for him, it involves not *just* the physical mark of circumcision but the total consecration of the heart towards God (as when Jesus says of Nathaniel in John 1.47, 'Here is a true Israelite; *no deceit is in him.*'[HCSB]) Such a view of circumcision here as an inward, rather than an outward work is nothing new, but is firmly rooted in the Old Testament:

The LORD your God will circumcise your hearts and the hearts of your descendants, so that you may love him with all your heart and with all your soul, and live. (Deut. 30.6)

Paul's belief that God's choice, rather than Jewish ancestry, determines who inherits salvation may have been a radical message within the Judaism of its time, but it was by no means unique. John the Baptist preached the same thing (Matt 3.7-10/Luke 3.7-9) and Jesus, as we have seen, expressed the same point in forceful terms to the centurion in Matthew chapter 8. Such ideas build on the many hints in the Old Testament prophetic books, particularly the latter sections of Isaiah, that Gentiles could be brought into a covenant relationship with God alongside Israel itself.

There is little basis on these grounds, therefore, for suggesting that Paul is somehow disowning his Jewish upbringing. To the Romans he writes that 'I am an Israelite myself, a descendant of Abraham, from the tribe of Benjamin' (11.1). Elsewhere in the letter he comments:

For I could wish that I myself were cursed and cut off from Christ for the sake of my people, those of my own race, the people of Israel. (Rom. 9.3-4)

This emphatic statement of identification with his own countrymen appears as deep and heartfelt as that of Moses (Ex. 32.32) or David (2 Sam. 24.17). Like them, his plea is, in effect, 'let the curse fall on me and spare the others', and he is under no illusions about the potential consequences of such a statement.

Furthermore, he continued even as a believer in Jesus to identify himself as a Pharisee (Acts 23.6) and maintained a belief in certain aspects of Jewish oral tradition. When, for instance, he describes the names of Pharaoh's magicians as Jannes and Jambres (2 Tim. 3.8) or talks of the rock the followed Moses in the wilderness (1 Cor. 10.4), he is referring to details absent from scripture but recorded in the Targums, Aramaic interpretations of the Old Testament that were only committed to writing much later.[1]

As a Pharisee, therefore, Paul's view of the Jewish law could hardly be a wholly negative one. While he is clear that such works of the law have no saving power in and of themselves, he can describe the law in very positive terms (Rom. 7.12; 1 Tim. 1.8-11) and exhorts Gentiles to fulfil its underlying principles (Rom. 13.10). He himself is acknowledged by the church in Jerusalem as 'living in obedience to the law' (Acts 21.24), a fact he later reaffirms himself (Acts 25.8), even if this stems from a sense of choice rather than obligation on his part (1 Cor. 9.20-21).

On occasions he is scrupulous to avoid giving offence to fellow Jews: he has Timothy circumcised in Acts 16.3 and on a later occasion is even willing to engage in a seven-day ritual cleansing, which would have culminated in a ceremonial sacrifice, in order to dispel false claims that he was encouraging Jews to abandon their ancestral traditions (Acts 21.20-26).[2] There is also possible evidence that he observed the Passover Feast and perhaps even exhorted his Gentile readers to do so (1 Cor. 5.7-8).

Elsewhere Paul teaches that the Jews retain their special privileges (Rom 3.1-2); they are still 'Israelites', keeping both the adoption and the covenants (9.4). They remain 'elect', chosen by God (11.28-29), and because of this belief in Messiah should come to them naturally (Rom. 11.24).

Nor does Paul expect Jewish believers to abandon their culture and tradition in embracing Christianity, but simply to accept Gentiles on the same terms if they wished to do the same:

Was a man already circumcised when he was called? He should not become uncircumcised. Was a man uncircumcised when he was called? He should not be circumcised. (1 Cor. 7.18)

As defensive as he is of Gentile freedom in his letter to the Galatians, Paul was also very insistent when writing to the Romans that Jews should not be forced to abandon their customs or act against their conscience:

Accept the one whose faith is weak, without quarrelling over disputable matters. One person's faith allows them to eat anything, but another, whose faith is weak, eats only vegetables. The one who eats everything must not treat with contempt the one who does not, and the one who does not eat everything must not judge the one who does, for God has accepted them. Who are you to judge someone else's servant? To their own master, servants stand or fall. And they will stand, for the Lord is able to make them stand.

One person considers one day more sacred than another; another considers every day alike. Each of them should be fully convinced in their own mind. Whoever regards one day as special does so to the Lord. Whoever eats meat does so to the Lord, for they give thanks to God; and whoever abstains does so to the Lord and gives thanks to God. ...

You, then, why do you judge your brother or sister? Or why do you treat them with contempt? For we will all stand before God's judgment seat. (Rom. 14.1-6, 10)

So has the church taken over God's purposes for the Jewish nation in Paul's understanding? We need to reflect carefully here. In 1 Corinthians 10.32 he *distinguishes* Jews, Gentiles and the church as three *separate* groups. And in Galatians 6.16, for all appearances to the contrary, he could be saying the same thing, since the NIV translation quoted earlier, which seems to *identify* the church with the 'Israel of God', omits the rather crucial word 'and' from the original Greek shown in bold type in the ESV version below:

And as for all who walk by this rule, peace and mercy be upon them, ***and*** upon the Israel of God. (ESV, similarly CEB, KJV, NASB, NET, NKJV, NRSV)[3]

Even if this passage, or Philippians 3, were truly to be implying that Christians have *replaced* physical 'Israel', the picture Paul has in mind is one that is very different from the church as we know it today. Rather, as in Romans, he sees a body in which both Jew and Gentile play an equal part, where Jews can legitimately choose to continue to follow the Mosaic law, and where Gentiles can only gain admission through adoption.

In any case, it is far from clear that Paul's main argument in Galatians is against Jewish Christians trying to force their practices on Gentiles, but rather against *Gentiles* who have received circumcision and are trying to persuade others to do the same, without understanding the implications of what they have done. In 6.13, he points out that 'even those who receive circumcision do not themselves keep the law' (RSV).

Could it be that by misreading Galatians as teaching a theology of replacement, large sections of the church, seeing themselves as the 'new Israel', have succumbed to the very kinds of ideas (drawn from the old covenant) that Paul was arguing against: circumcision (reinstituted as infant baptism), an ordained priesthood, special days and seasons, and so on? If so, one set of laws has simply been replaced by another!

The problem arises from our failure to take in the much fuller perspective on the relationship between Jews and Gentiles set out in Chapter 11 of Paul's letter to the Romans. Here, leading up to his conclusion that God's gifts and his call are irrevocable (v. 29), he asks:

Did God reject his people? By no means! I am an Israelite myself, a descendant of Abraham, from the tribe of Benjamin. God did not reject his people, whom he foreknew. ... Rather, because of their transgression, salvation has come to the Gentiles to make Israel envious [*note that 'Gentiles' are clearly distinguished from 'Israel' here.*] But if their transgression means riches for the world, and their loss means riches for the Gentiles, how much greater riches will their full inclusion bring!
(Rom. 11.1-2, 11-12)

To develop this picture further, he uses an image drawn from olive cultivation, with which many of his hearers may have been familiar:

If some of the branches have been broken off, and you, though a wild olive shoot, have been grafted in among the others and now share in the nourishing sap from the olive root, do not consider yourself to be superior to those other branches. If you do, consider this: you do not support the root, but the root supports you... And if they do not persist in unbelief, they will be grafted in, for God is able to graft them in again. After all, if you were cut out of an olive tree that is wild by nature, and contrary to nature were grafted into a cultivated olive tree, how much more readily will these, the natural branches, be grafted into their own olive tree! (Rom. 11.17-18, 23-24)

Paul goes on to talk about a 'mystery' that 'Israel has experienced a hardening in part until the full number of the Gentiles has come in, and in this way *all Israel* will be saved' (11.25-26), and the verses he quotes from the Old Testament to illustrate this make clear that by 'all Israel' he means natural, physical Israel:

'The deliverer will come from Zion;
  he will turn godlessness away from Jacob.
And this is my covenant with them
  when I take away their sins.'
      (Rom. 11.26-27; cf. Is. 59.20, 21; Jer. 31.33, 34)

Part of the difficulty for us in assessing all these different passages today is that Paul so often varied his tone and his message according to the nature of his audience. This is very apparent in Acts, where arguments he used when debating with Jews and Gentiles are very different in content from one another. The same seems to be true in his epistles: in his letter to Rome, where large numbers of Jews had accepted Jesus as their Messiah, his tone is measured and his arguments are nuanced and carefully calibrated. On the other hand, when talking to Gentile-dominated congregations like those of Galatia or Philippi, he can be much more brash and outspoken in his language.

However, in one letter clearly directed at a largely Gentile audience, Paul takes the argument he makes in chapters 9 to 11 of Romans a stage further. In the second part of chapter 2 of Ephesians, Paul begins by discussing the status of Gentiles cut off from divine favour. Outside the scope of God's kingdom, they are 'separate from Christ, excluded from citizenship in Israel and foreigners to the covenants of the promise, without hope and without God in the world' (2.12). But through the death of Jesus on the cross the 'dividing wall of hostility' between Jew and Gentile has finally been taken away, so that 'now in Christ Jesus you who once were far away have been brought near by the blood of Christ' (2.13-14).

As he did in Romans, then, Paul is able to write here of a 'mystery', which is in this case that 'through the gospel the Gentiles are *heirs together* with Israel, *members together* of one body, and *sharers together* in the promise in Christ Jesus' (3.6). If Paul is able to wax lyrical in his letter to Rome about the 'greater riches' such a combination of Jews and Gentiles would produce, even 'life from the dead' (Rom. 11.13-15), his description in Ephesians is even more lavish, talking of 'one new humanity' that would emerge (2.15). Such a plan, 'which for ages past was kept hidden in God' (3.9), results in extraordinary consequences that are cosmic in their scope, so that 'the manifold wisdom of God should be made known to the rulers and authorities in the heavenly realms' (3.10).

The obvious conclusion to draw from this passage and from chapters 9 to 11 of Romans is that God's purposes for Israel are very far from finished in Paul's thinking and, indeed, are central to the future of the church. As Gentile believers, we have been drawn into a plan of salvation which began with Jews, which centres on a Jew, and which involves the Jews right through to the end. As C.E.B. Cranfield points out,

It is only where the Church persists in refusing to learn this message, where it secretly - perhaps quite unconsciously - believes that its own existence is based on human achievement, and so fails to understand God's mercy to itself, that it is unable to believe in God's mercy for still unbelieving Israel, and so entertains the ugly and unscriptural notion that God has cast off His people Israel and simply replaced it by the Christian Church. These three chapters [Rom. 9-11] emphatically forbid us to speak of the Church as having once and for all taken the place of the Jewish people.[4]

Using Paul's writings to create a 'dividing wall of hostility' between Jew and Gentile is the diametric opposite of his real intentions, which is that through Christ's death we should 'both have access to the Father by one Spirit' (Eph. 2.18). There are important lessons that the church still needs to learn from this. In the next chapter we will follow through Paul's arguments to see the vital implications his thinking still holds for us today.

For the one-time Pharisee Saul of Tarsus, of course, reaching such conclusions marks a huge, almost unimaginable leap forward in his journey of faith. Once the arch-persecutor of the church, he now becomes a trailblazer for the universal scope of the gospel. Yet in doing so, he never fully abandons his Hebrew roots. Rather, in being 'all things to all people' (1 Cor. 9.22) he demonstrates the 'one new humanity' which marks the crowning summit of his gospel message. For Paul reconciliation between Jew and Gentile stands not just as an aspiration but as a crowning objective in God's plan, the culmination of history itself, when 'all Israel will be saved' (Rom. 11.26). It is small wonder that Paul concludes Romans 11, at the end of his longest and most systematic discussion of the relationship between Jews and Gentiles, with an outburst of exuberant praise:

Oh, the depth of the riches of the wisdom and knowledge of God!
    How unsearchable his judgments,
    and his paths beyond tracing out!
    'Who has known the mind of the Lord?
    Or who has been his counsellor?'
    'Who has ever given to God,
    that God should repay them?'
    For from him and through him and for him are all things.
    To him be the glory for ever! Amen. (Rom. 11.33-36)

# 9 SHARING THE BLESSING

In the last four chapters we considered what the principal writers of the New Testament are saying about the relationship between Israel and the church. Now we need to put the pieces of the jigsaw back together. How do God's purposes for Gentile and Jew fit with each other? What conclusions can we draw from the Old Testament itself? And what are the practical consequences for us today?

We started our exploration of God's purposes for Israel and the church in Chapter One with a reflection on the story of Rachel and Leah. Despite the intense rivalry that separates the two sisters, they are bonded together by a common destiny which is ultimately far greater than the division between them, and finally speak together with a common voice.

For all its suggestive parallels, however, there is nothing *specific* in this story that relates to the relationship between Jews and Gentiles. For a much clearer signpost in the Old Testament, we need to travel forward to another 'two brides' story in the Old Testament, which occurs at a significant later juncture in the nation's history.

Naomi is in exile in Moab, having been forced to leave Israel because of famine. During this time she loses not just her husband but also her grown-up children. With nothing left to stay for, she hears that the situation has improved back in her homeland and decides to return.

Naomi has two Moabite daughters-in-law, the widows of her two sons. She urges them to remain behind as she is convinced that they will have no future in Israel. Orpah eventually agrees to return but Ruth replies as follows:

'Don't urge me to leave you or to turn back from you. Where you go I will go, and where you stay I will stay. Your people will be my people and your God my God. Where you die I will die, and there I will be buried. May the LORD deal with me, be it ever so severely, if even death separates you and me.'

(Ruth 1.16-17)

Ruth's decision is potentially a costly one, knowing that she may never be able to marry again (vv. 11-13). Nevertheless, she steps out in faith, convinced that she is doing God's will.

Despite the bleak outlook, Ruth has one thing on her side: initiative. Having little else to occupy herself with, she offers to collect leftover grain that the reapers have ignored from nearby fields, in order to feed Naomi and herself. This act of humble service attracts the notice of Naomi's wealthy kinsman, Boaz, and ultimately leads to her becoming his wife. As a result of her faith and her obedience she becomes not just the ancestor of King David but of Jesus himself.

The story of Ruth is full of powerful symbolism. Her gathering of discarded grain reminds us of the Canaanite woman in the gospels, who symbolically gathers 'the crumbs that fall from [her] master's table', gaining access to Jesus through her boldness (Matt. 15.27). Like this unnamed woman, Ruth is a Gentile outsider who has 'come to take refuge' under the wings of 'the LORD, the God of Israel' (Ruth 2.12). Through God's grace, Ruth herself is honoured by the citizens of Bethlehem as a Gentile with a status equal to Rachel and Leah, the great matriarchs of Israel's history (4.11).

Here, then, is a perfect picture of God's plan of salvation which reinforces what we read in the last chapter. In Romans we saw Paul trying to demonstrate how Gentiles can come in from the cold and be 'grafted in' to the promises of Israel: how we, as 'a wild olive shoot', are able to 'share in the nourishing sap from the olive root' (Rom. 11.17). In Ephesians we saw how likewise how the Gentiles, originally 'separate from Christ, excluded from citizenship in Israel and foreigners to the covenants of the promise' have now been 'brought near by the blood of Christ' (Eph. 2.12-13).

The key image in both cases is that of *inclusion*, not *replacement*. This reflects the words of Paul's initial commission to witness to the Gentiles, 'to open their eyes and turn them from darkness to light, and from the power of Satan to God, so that they may receive forgiveness of sins and ***a place among*** those who are sanctified by faith in me' (Acts 26.18). The language of Christ's call to Paul is clear: rather than *supplanting* or *overthrowing* what has already been established, the Gentiles will be *brought in* to what is already in existence.

A similar idea emerges from the revolutionary vision that Peter has in the first part of Acts. Peter sees a huge sheet being lowered from heaven three times, containing 'all kinds of four-footed animals, as well as reptiles and birds'. He then hears a voice telling him, 'Get up, Peter. Kill and eat.' He replies, 'Surely not, Lord! I have never eaten anything impure or unclean.' The Lord tells him a second time, 'Do not call anything impure that God has made clean' (Acts 10.11-16).

Though clearly of momentous significance, this encounter is often misunderstood. It does not imply that God's favour has somehow been *exchanged* from one people-group to another. The 'unclean' animals now deemed acceptable to eat do not *displace* those previously considered as 'clean'. Rather, they are brought into the *same* category and degree of 'cleanness' as the others. It is this image of 'bringing in' to an enlarged sphere of blessing that remains uppermost for Luke in Acts and Paul in Romans.

As we noted in Chapter Three, this pattern of inclusion is one we find repeatedly in the Old Testament. In Ezekiel 47.22 'the foreigners residing among you' are to be considered as 'native-born Israelites; *along with you* they are to be allotted an inheritance among the tribes of Israel.' The same theme is echoed in Solomon's prayer for the temple in 1 Kings 8.41-43:

'As for the foreigner who does not belong to your people Israel but has come from a distant land because of your name – for they will hear of your great name and your mighty hand and your outstretched arm – when they come and pray towards this temple, then hear from heaven, your dwelling-place. Do whatever the foreigner asks of you, so that all the peoples of the earth may know your name and fear you, as do your own people Israel, and may know that this house I have built bears your Name'.

Similarly, we read in Isaiah that

The LORD will have compassion on Jacob;
  once again he will choose Israel
  and will settle them in their own land.
*Foreigners will join them*
  *and unite with the descendants of Jacob.* (14.1)

Later in Isaiah this idea is developed further through a wonderful sequence of images. In chapter 52, God promises to redeem Jerusalem, accomplishing this in chapter 53 through the death of the servant who bears the sin of the entire nation. In chapter 54 we see the unconditional covenant of peace between God and Israel that results from this, with Zion being told to 'enlarge the place of your tent' (v. 2). This theme is developed in chapter 55, where Israel is told that 'you will summon nations you know not, and nations you do not know will come running to you' (v. 5).

In the following chapter, the invitation is broadened still further:

Let no foreigner who is bound to the LORD say,
   'The LORD will surely exclude me from his people.' …

For this is what the LORD says:

'To the eunuchs who keep my Sabbaths,
   who choose what pleases me
   and hold fast to my covenant –
to them I will give within my temple and its walls
   a memorial and a name
   better than sons and daughters;
I will give them an everlasting name
   that will endure for ever.
And foreigners who bind themselves to the LORD
   to minister to him,
to love the name of the LORD,
   and to be his servants,
all who keep the Sabbath without desecrating it
   and who hold fast to my covenant –
these I will bring to my holy mountain
   and give them joy in my house of prayer.
Their burnt offerings and sacrifices
   will be accepted on my altar;
for my house will be called
   a house of prayer for all nations.'
The Sovereign LORD declares –
   he who gathers the exiles of Israel:
'I will gather still others to them
   besides those already gathered.' (Is 56.3-8)

It is the last verse of this passage, among others, that Jesus seems to be echoing when he says in John 10.16:

'I have other sheep that are not of this sheepfold. I must bring them also. They too will listen to my voice, and there shall be one flock and one shepherd.'

The consistent testimony of scripture, therefore, is that although the identity of the people of God centres primarily on the nation of Israel itself it can, by incorporation, be extended to the Gentiles. For this reason Paul can tell the (Gentile) Corinthians that '*our* ancestors [in Exodus] were all under the cloud and that they all passed through the sea' (1 Cor. 10.1).

As adopted children, in other words, we can fully participate in the spiritual blessings, unique calling and divine protection accorded to God's people in the Old Testament. Thus Peter can describe us as 'a chosen people, a royal priesthood, a holy nation, God's special possession' (1 Peter 2.9) using terms originally applying to Israel in the Old Testament (Ex. 19.5-6; Deut. 7.6).[1]

By the same token, however, it is only through God's *existing* promises to Israel that this becomes possible. It is easy to forget that the new covenant which Jesus inaugurates at the Last Supper is one that in Jeremiah 31 is promised *specifically* to Israel and Judah, as we pointed out in Chapter Three. It was initially one made *by a Jew* with *other Jews*. We as Gentiles participate as guests, not as substitutes or replacements. As the great Swiss theologian Karl Barth writes,

The Gentile Christian community of every age and of every land is a guest in the House of Israel. It assumes the election and calling of Israel. It lives in fellowship with the King of Israel.[2]

The good news of the gospel, therefore, is revolutionary, and yet firmly anchored in the Old Testament. God's invitation is extended to the Gentiles, who are able to take an equal place in his kingdom, as heirs *together with* [as opposed to 'instead of'] Israel (Eph. 3.6). If the church is a replacement in any sense, therefore, it is a *Jewish* replacement into which all (including the Gentiles) can be included, replacing an Israel from which the 'unclean' (Jewish or Gentile) were *excluded.*

Yet throughout the Old Testament there is a clear order of precedence in this scheme of things: salvation comes **first** to the Jews and only **afterwards** to the Gentiles. This pattern continues consistently into the New, as the following verses show:

The woman was a Greek, born in Syrian Phoenicia. She begged Jesus to drive the demon out of her daughter. '*First* let the children eat all they want,' he told her, 'for it is not right to take the children's bread and toss it to the dogs.' (Mark 7.26-27)

'When God raised up his servant, he sent him *first* to you to bless you by turning each of you from your wicked ways.' (Acts 3.26)

Then Paul and Barnabas answered them boldly: 'We had to speak the word of God to you *first*. Since you reject it and do not consider yourselves worthy of eternal life, we now turn to the Gentiles. (Acts 13.46)

When Silas and Timothy came from Macedonia, Paul devoted himself exclusively to preaching, testifying to the *Jews* that Jesus was the Messiah. But when they opposed Paul and became abusive, he shook out his clothes in protest and said to them, 'Your blood be on your own heads! I am innocent of it. From now on I will go to the *Gentiles*.' (Acts 18.5-6)

I am saying nothing beyond what the prophets and Moses said would happen – that the Messiah would suffer and, as the first to rise from the dead, would bring the message of light to his own people *and* to the Gentiles.' (Acts 26.22-23)

Three days later he called together the local *Jewish* leaders. ... Some were convinced by what he said, but others would not believe. They disagreed among themselves and began to leave after Paul had made this final statement ... 'I want you to know that God's salvation has been sent to the *Gentiles,* and they will listen!' (Acts 28.17, 24-25, 28)

For I am not ashamed of the gospel, because it is the power of God that brings salvation to everyone who believes: *first* to the *Jew*, then to the *Gentile*. (Rom. 1.16)

There will be trouble and distress for every human being who does evil: *first* for the *Jew*, then for the *Gentile*; but glory, honour and peace for everyone who does good: *first* for the *Jew*, then for the *Gentile*. (Rom. 2.9-10)

What if he did this to make the riches of his glory known to the objects of his mercy, whom he prepared in advance for glory – even us, whom he also called, *not only* from the *Jews but also* from the *Gentiles*? (Rom. 9.23-24)

For I tell you that Christ has become a servant of the *Jews* on behalf of God's truth, so that the promises made to the patriarchs might be confirmed and, moreover, that the *Gentiles* might glorify God for his mercy. (Rom. 15.8-9)

All these passages suggest that, even under the New Covenant, the Jews have not lost their central role in God's purposes. Our participation as Gentiles comes entirely through God's grace and rests solely in Jesus' death on the cross. The marginalisation of the Jews by the church throughout history, far from demonstrating this, represents the total opposite of the kingdom Jesus was inaugurating.

In Ephesians 2.12-13 Paul makes the matter abundantly clear. As we saw earlier, he tells Gentile believers who were once 'separate from Christ, excluded from citizenship in Israel and foreigners to the covenants of the promise' that they are now 'brought near by the blood of Christ'. The wording here is highly significant. Far from suggesting that the Jews need to leave behind their Jewishness in order to embrace Jesus, as the church has so tragically insisted for the last two thousand years, the passage suggests rather that we as Gentiles need to affirm the vision and calling of Israel for us to be fully plumbed in to the life-giving supply of God's covenant promises to the Jews, which are centred on the coming of the Messiah himself.

It is important to recognise that within this shared blessing, however, Jew and Gentile are able to maintain their distinctive identities. Nowhere is there any suggestion that we should all be subsumed into a single uniform whole. For proof of such diversity, we need look no further than the New Testament itself. While much of it is directed primarily at a Gentile audience, it also embraces material of a very different tone and substance, such as the letter of James, so clearly aimed at Jewish readers in its style, language and practical wisdom.

In this context it is worth noting how the Council of Jerusalem in Acts 15, while waiving the detailed requirements of the Law for Gentiles, did not abandon it for Jews. Indeed, Acts 21 records that when Paul returned to Jerusalem, 'James and all the elders' of the church, while rejoicing at the harvest among the Gentiles, point out that 'many thousands of Jews have believed, and *all of them are zealous for the law*' (vv. 18, 20).

Such a divergence of practice between Jew and Gentile under a single umbrella was by no means unprecedented. It can be found in Jeremiah 35 where the Rechabites, the descendants of Moses' father-in-law Jethro, are commended for maintaining their distinctive life-style. In the same way, as we saw in the last chapter, Paul instructs the Jewish and Gentile believers in Rome that they do not need to conform to identical laws of conscience, but are free to maintain the practices which they feel individually in their spirits are right before God.

Nor should we read too much into Paul's implication that those who desire to live within a more restrictive set of laws are 'weak' in faith (Rom. 14.1-2). For Paul, 'weakness' and 'strength' can mean something opposite to what the world might understand by such terms (2 Cor. 12.10). Those who feel that Jews need to renounce a steadfast adherence to Old Testament law in order to come to faith in Christ should remember the words of Jesus in Matthew chapter 5:

'Do not think that I have come to abolish the Law or the Prophets; I have not come to abolish them but to fulfil them. For truly I tell you, until heaven and earth disappear, not the smallest letter, not the least stroke of a pen, will by any means disappear from the Law until everything is accomplished. Therefore *anyone who sets aside one of the least of these commands and teaches others accordingly will be called least in the kingdom of heaven, but whoever practises and teaches these commands will be called great in the kingdom of heaven.* (vv. 17-19)

For us this means that, even in the kingdom of heaven, where salvation comes through unmerited grace alone, those who choose to live free from the Law ('the least') must defer to those ('the great') whose conscience enjoins them to keep it (remembering that for Jesus, too, 'greatest' and 'least' are interchangeable positions [Luke 22.26-27]).

As Christians, there are several things that we can learn from this 'live-and-let-live' approach. Firstly, we need to celebrate each other's differences. This is just as important *within* the Gentile church as it is when we consider Messianic fellowships established by Jews themselves. At one extreme, many of us have either looked down on other Christian denominations or even demonised them. At the other extreme, some have considered all such differences of tradition to be a curse, rather than a rich blessing to be celebrated and shared, one that reflects the diversity inherent in God's own nature and the world he has created. Those who carry a self-righteous pride in having broken away from the 'dead' tradition of earlier forms of church should remember that Paul's teaching on the relationship between Jews and Gentiles is valid in a purely Gentile context too:

Do not consider yourself to be superior to those other branches. If you do, consider this: *you do not support the root, but the root supports you.* (Rom. 11.18).

In the same way, those from traditional mainline churches who look askance at their doctrinally 'loose' and apparently 'irreverent' brethren should remember Luke's parable of the Pharisee in the temple (18.9-14), whose 'holier-than-thou' attitude towards the tax collector earns him no favour from the Lord. We need to learn to accept each other, love each other, forgive each other, just as the Lord loves us. As Paul says to the Philippians,

Do nothing from rivalry or conceit, but *in humility count others more significant than yourselves*. (Phil. 2.3 ESV)

True unity, in other words, does not flow out from a 'top-down' conformism, but from a real humility and brokenness before God. In the past, so much of our interaction has been rooted in mutual fear, suspicion and recrimination. We need to reach out to each other in love and trust.

This applies not just across denominations, but across cultural boundaries as well. In the past the church has attempted to extend God's kingdom by planting carbon copies of Western culture in very different contexts. In the end, this amounts to little more than cultural imperialism. Why should a Muslim who comes to Christ, for example, not continue praying five times a day, or washing his hands before he reads the Bible? Why should a Buddhist who comes to Christ not continue meditating on the promises and person of Jesus?

By the same token, we should not expect a Jew who comes to Jesus to swallow two thousand years of non-Jewish and sometimes anti-Jewish tradition lock, stock and barrel. A Christian visitor to a Messianic fellowship from a relatively traditional background may be disturbed to find no visual depiction of the cross, no recitation of the Nicene creed, and the meeting taking place on a Saturday rather than on a Sunday. A Christian from one of the newer generations of churches might, on the other hand, be challenged by the lack of mention of the name 'Jesus', the use of unfamiliar words and phrases, and elements of liturgy and tradition that seem out of place. And certainly there would be no bacon rolls beforehand!

True freedom offers us the choice to embrace customs and rules as well as to reject them. If it is fine for a Christian to celebrate Christmas, to wear a wedding ring (a pagan symbol of wholeness) or to go on a low-fat diet, then why should a Jewish believer in Christ not be free to celebrate Hanukkah (like Christmas, a festival not prescribed in the Bible and yet which Jesus also observes in John 10), to wear a prayer shawl or to follow kosher food laws?

Clearly we must move on beyond the 'one-size-fits-all' mentality that has controlled so much of our thinking in the past. Paul's picture of 'one body, many parts' provides a perfect model of how believers in the Lord, whether Jewish or Gentile, can maintain their unique characteristics and yet still function together.[3] The relationships between the members of the Trinity provide an ideal picture here: one God in three distinct persons who share the same spiritual DNA and who act together in perfect unity and harmony.

Jesus' prayer for both his (Jewish) disciples and the (Jewish and Gentile) believers who receive him through their witness, that 'all of them may be one' (John 17.21), just as he is one with the Father, shows how this same pattern needs to work for believers as well.

This New Testament understanding of 'church' in which Jew and Gentile could preserve their distinctive character is highlighted in Galatians 3.28, where Paul draws a parallel between Jew and Gentile on the one hand and male and female on the other, who preserve distinct but complementary roles.

Such a parallel, when laid alongside the mysterious union which Paul alludes to in chapter 2 of Ephesians of 'one new humanity' in Christ, might suggest Jews and Gentiles are fundamentally incomplete without each other, just as Adam was incomplete without Eve, who was taken from his rib. Only by bringing them together can God's purpose for the human race be fully achieved.

Unity of this kind, however, comes at a price. Paul, in exhorting the Philippians to adopt an attitude of complete humility towards one other, points to the example of Christ,

who, being in very nature God,
    did not consider equality with God something to be used to his
own advantage;
rather, he made himself nothing
    by taking the very nature of a servant,
    being made in human likeness.
And being found in appearance as a man,
    he humbled himself

by becoming obedient to death –
  even death on a cross! (Phil. 2.6-8)

In all these things, a helpful example is provided by the
story of Ruth that we considered earlier. Wholeheartedly,
she is willing to identify herself with the sufferings of the
Jewish people, no matter what the personal cost to herself.

Throughout history, when the church has been faced with a
very similar choice, only a few have copied Ruth's
example. For some in the past, the decision to nail one's
colours to the same mast as our Jewish comrades has been
a very difficult one. For Christians in Nazi Germany, most
took the easy route. A few, however, had the courage to
say, like Ruth, 'Your people will be my people'. In some
cases, this led to imprisonment, torture and even death.

What about us? Today, without being under that same
intense pressure, we are still faced with that same basic
choice. Naomi tells both widows to go away as a test. Only
one stays. Many of us, like Orpah, will choose to go our
own way, turning our back on our historic family ties with
Judaism, untramelled by our deep roots in the past.
Alternatively, like Ruth, we may choose to cleave to Israel
and to treasure our joint Judaeo-Christian heritage.

In the end, it was Ruth's determination to stick with the
Jewish people, come what may, which led to her becoming
the great-grandmother of King David and ultimately to her
having a place in the family tree of Jesus. Perhaps there is a
lesson here for us, too. We can either stand as an innocent
bystander in the corridor of history, like Orpah, or take a

real slice in the action, like Ruth. But in the end, it is the bride that stays with Israel who is the one who paves the way for the coming of Jesus.

# 10 A GLORIOUS FUTURE

It was a short letter penned by King Cyrus of Persia, preserved for us at the beginning of the book of Ezra, which changed the direction of the Old Testament, enabling some of the exiled Jews of Babylon to return to Jerusalem and rebuild the temple which had been razed to the ground by the Babylonians in 586 BC. Without that letter history as we know it might have been very different.

Some 2,500 years later another brief letter was to impact the future in a similarly powerful way. Written by the British Foreign Secretary Arthur Balfour to the wealthy Jewish financier Lord Rothschild on November 2nd 1917, it declared that 'His Majesty's government view with favour the establishment in Palestine of a national home for the Jewish people'.[1]

The timing of the decision made by the British cabinet two days earlier could not have been more striking. Exactly four hundred years to the very day since Martin Luther had triggered the countdown to the Reformation by nailing his theses to the door of the cathedral in Wittenberg, opening the door to a re-evaluation of scripture which inevitably included a reassessment of God's promises to Israel, the wartime government's choice marked the first time in over two and a half millennia that a major world power had enabled a return of the Jews to their ancestral home.

It was also very close to four hundred years since Jerusalem had first come under Ottoman rule. It is intriguing, therefore, that the very moment the cabinet voted unanimously for a Jewish national homeland, Allied troops broke the strategic stalemate in the First World War at Beersheba, the very place where God had appeared to Jacob during his final farewell to the Promised Land thousands of years earlier and promised that Israel would one day become a great nation (Gen. 46.3). Exactly one year later to the very day hostilities between Britain and the Turks ceased. Within a short time, Herbert Samuel, appointed high commissioner from Palestine from 1921 to 1925, became the first Jew in charge of the land for two thousand years.

It was not the first time that such a return had been suggested. After his attempted invasion of Israel in 1799 Napoleon had planned to allow the Jews to return but the British and Turks outmanoeuvred him. During the nineteenth century, however, influential social reformers such as Wilberforce and Lord Shaftesbury as well as

Christian leaders like Charles Spurgeon and Bishop J. C. Ryle had argued much more persuasively for a restoration of the Jews to their ancestral homeland. Under Shaftesbury's influence, the Jewish-born Anglican, Michael Solomon Alexander, a former Rabbi, became the first Protestant bishop in Jerusalem. Another Anglican clergyman, William Hechler, used his influence to gain access for Theodor Herzl, the founder of modern Zionism, into the highest corridors of power in Europe.

Behind many of these aspirations lay a firm belief in the Old Testament prophecies of a return of the Jews to Israel. And while not the only factor involved, such an ideal may have played a significant part in the framing of the Balfour Declaration. A number of the leading decision-makers in the British cabinet of 1917, including David Lloyd George, Arthur Balfour and Jan Smuts, were from evangelical Christian backgrounds which promoted a respect for the Bible's teaching on Israel, as was the American President Woodrow Wilson, who was also supportive of the plan. It seemed that, for the first time in many centuries, history and Biblical promises were beginning to intersect. As Winston Churchill later declared,

we committed ourselves to the idea that some day, somehow, far off in the future...there might well be a great Jewish State there, numbered by millions, far exceeding the present inhabitants of the country.[2]

They would have been aware, however, that the Bible goes far beyond merely predicting the return of the Jews to the Promised Land. Although the Old Testament was written against the backdrop of a Gentile-dominated world, Israel's unique and essential calling at the centre of nations points to something far greater. Through the later prophetic writings such as Isaiah and Daniel we discover that Gentile control of the world will ultimately come to an end and be replaced by God's own direct rule from Jerusalem itself. Jesus himself referred to a 'times of the Gentiles' as a transitional period in Israel's history (Luke 21.24).

The end result of this process is very far from being Israel's rejection, abandonment or replacement. Instead, she gains a place of high honour: the Gentile nations come bowing before her. Jerusalem remains central to the earthly kingdom of God, as we see, for example, in chapter 8 of Zechariah:

This is what the LORD Almighty says: 'Many peoples and the inhabitants of many cities will yet come, and the inhabitants of one city will go to another and say, "Let us go at once to entreat the LORD and seek the LORD Almighty. I myself am going." And many peoples and powerful nations will come to Jerusalem to seek the LORD Almighty and to entreat him.'

This is what the LORD Almighty says: 'In those days ten people from all languages and nations will take firm hold of one Jew by the hem of his robe and say, "Let us go with you, because we have heard that God is with you."' (Zech. 8.20-23)

It is also noteworthy that the Jewish ceremonial feasts, far from disappearing, acquire a universal significance:

'From one New Moon to another and from one Sabbath to another, all mankind will come and bow down before me,' says the LORD. (Is. 66.23)

Then the survivors from all the nations that have attacked Jerusalem will go up year after year to worship the King, the LORD Almighty, and to celebrate the Festival of Tabernacles. (Zech. 14.16)

The progressive revelation of the Old Testament in charting the steadily enlarging horizons of God's purposes is summed up beautifully in Chapter 49 of Isaiah, where the calling of Israel and her Messiah partly overlap, as we saw in Chapter Three. As we noted then, the revelation increases gradually: at first, the servant *is* Israel itself (v. 3); then he is sent *to* Israel (v. 5), before finally being sent to the world (v. 6):

He said to me, 'You are my servant,
   Israel, in whom I will display my splendour.' ...

And now the LORD says –
   he who formed me in the womb to be his servant
to bring Jacob back to him
   and gather Israel to himself,
for I am honoured in the eyes of the LORD
   and my God has been my strength –
he says:
'It is too small a thing for you to be my servant
   to restore the tribes of Jacob
   and bring back those of Israel I have kept.
I will also make you a light for the Gentiles,
   that my salvation may reach to the ends of the earth.'

Yet it is clear that Israel remains the *primary* context of the servant's mission, and the Gentiles are embraced only as an extension to this (v. 6), with a firm distinction maintained between the two. Furthermore, an important part of the servant's function is to *re-gather* the tribes of Israel, a fact

154

underlined later on in the passage, where the Gentiles are called upon to assist:

See, I have engraved you on the palms of my hands;
   your walls are ever before me.
Your children hasten back,
   and those who laid you waste depart from you. ...

This is what the Sovereign LORD says:

'See, I will beckon to the nations,
   I will lift up my banner to the peoples;
they will bring your sons in their arms
   and carry your daughters on their hips.
Kings will be your foster fathers,
   and their queens your nursing mothers.
They will bow down before you with their faces to the ground;
   they will lick the dust at your feet.
Then you will know that I am the LORD;
   those who hope in me will not be disappointed.'
(vv. 16-17, 22-23)

Throughout Isaiah the ultimate stature of Israel within God's overall purposes is steadily amplified and enlarged. The law of God will go out from Jerusalem, and all nations will stream to the temple (2.2-3); universal peace will be established from Israel to the nations (2.4; 9.7); the Messiah will reign on David's throne in justice and righteousness (9.7; 11.1-4); he will slay the wicked with the breath of his lips (11.4); ecosystems will be transformed (11.6-9); the nations will rally to him and Jewish exiles will return (11.10-12); the blind will see and the deaf will hear (32.3). In the latter part of the book the vision intensifies: Israel will be exalted among the nations and wealth will pour into her; she will be filled with the glory and righteousness of God, and people will live to extraordinary ages (chapters 60-62; 65-66). The other Old Testament prophetic books develop and extend these themes in a variety of ways.

Only by hermeneutical gymnastics of breathtaking agility can all these promises be legitimately transferred away from Israel to the church. Such a reassignment could only be made possible by completely re-writing large sections of the Old Testament and discarding a wealth of specific geographical references which leave us in no doubt that the Jews are the clear recipient of the blessings. While the coming of Jesus in the New Testament might dramatically enlarge the scope of God's covenant plans, the hope such promises offer to Israel are by no means set aside. On the contrary, the future restoration of the nation remains, arguably, central to Jesus' thinking.

A clear hint at this firm expectation for a reconstituted nation can be seen in Jesus' remark in Matthew 19.28, which clearly refers back to the servant's commission in Isaiah 49.6-12 to *restore* the land and to *re-gather* the Jewish people:

'Truly I tell you, *at the renewal of all things*, when the Son of Man sits on his glorious throne, you who have followed me will also sit on twelve thrones, judging *the twelve tribes of Israel*.

According to E. P. Sanders, this passage 'confirms the view that Jesus looked for the restoration of Israel'.[3] A similar suggestion may well be present earlier when Jesus says that 'Elijah comes and *will restore all things*' (Matt. 17.11).

While partly in context referring to the ministry of John the Baptist, he must inevitably have been looking forward to a more comprehensive fulfilment in the future.

If so, when Jesus preaches the good news of the kingdom of God (Matt. 4.23, 9.35; Luke 4.43, 8.1) and sends the disciples out with same message (Matt. 10.7/Luke 9.2; 9.60, 10.9, 10.11), the Old Testament promises of a renewed Israel and a renewed earth may well have been central in his thinking, both as a future reality and one that actively invades the present. This clearly builds on a tension already present in the Old Testament: while the kingdom of God is a present reality (Num. 23.21, Ps. 145.10-13), it is also a future hope (Dan. 2.44, 7.14, 7.27, Zech. 14.9).

Luke in particular seems to carry a consciousness of this: Simeon was 'waiting for the consolation of Israel' (2.25); the prophetess Anna speaks to 'all who were looking forward to the redemption of Jerusalem' (2.38); the people near Jerusalem thought mistakenly 'that the kingdom of God was going to appear at once' (19.11); Jesus tells his disciples to 'lift up your heads, because your redemption is drawing near' (21.28); he will not eat the Passover again 'until it finds fulfilment in the kingdom of God' (Luke 22.15-16); Joseph of Arimathea is described also as 'waiting for the kingdom of God' (23.51).

Against this background, the question the disciples put to Jesus in Acts 1.6 makes perfect sense:

'Lord, are you at this time going to restore the kingdom to Israel?'

Far from being the result of futile and misguided speculation, such a question might well have been a reasoned response to teaching Jesus had given them, both during his earthly ministry, and in the forty days after his resurrection, when he 'spoke about the kingdom of God' (Acts 1.3). Although we know little about this post-resurrection teaching, we do know that he said '*everything* must be fulfilled that is written about me in the Law of Moses, the Prophets and the Psalms' and that he 'opened their minds so they could understand the Scriptures' (Luke 24.44-45). This 'everything' must surely have included the clear promise, already noted, that the Messiah would one day rule as king on David's throne (Is. 9.7; Ezek. 37.24-25), and return the land to Israel's possession (Is. 49.8). Such an understanding would help to explain much more easily Peter's declaration to the crowd in Jerusalem in Acts 3.21 about 'the time ... for God to *restore everything*, as he promised long ago through his holy prophets.'

Paul may also have been alluding to such a physical, earthly, rule of Christ when he writes that

Then the end will come, *when he hands over the kingdom* to God the Father after he has destroyed all dominion, authority and power. For *he must reign until he has put all his enemies under his feet.*                                    (1 Cor. 15.24-25)

In Revelation the same expectation appears: after the seventh angel sounds his trumpet, the voices in heaven declare:

'The kingdom of the world has become
the kingdom of our Lord and of his Messiah,
and he will reign for ever and ever.' (Rev. 11.15)

Likewise Revelation 20 talks about those who 'came to life and reigned with Christ a thousand years', pointing to an intermediate earthly state short of the new heaven and new earth that are to follow.

All along, however, the New Testament writers have to wrestle with an apparent problem. The Jews have, by and large, rejected their Messiah, and the promised blessings have only partially materialised. Certain events, such as the lowering of the sailsheet in Acts 10, seem to invite a dramatic reinterpretation of the Old Testament. Has God suddenly changed course? Has the old crew been replaced? Is the destination now different?

In order to answer this question, Paul appears to build on clues in Isaiah, where Israel has to overcome a God-ordained blindness and deafness (6.10, 29.10, 42.18-19). Only when God acts unilaterally do the blind begin to see again (29.18, 32.3). Against this background, he can write in 2 Corinthians 3.14-15 of a veil over the Jewish people which will only be taken away in Christ. Likewise, in Romans 11, the temporary blindness that has come over Israel makes it possible for the full number of Gentiles to be saved (vv. 8, 10, 25).

This idea is also significant for Luke, as we saw in Chapter Six. Both in his gospel and in Acts he sees the Jewish rejection of Jesus as a temporary one which will in time be completely overturned. Ultimately God will reveal the identity of the Messiah in a manner that is unmistakable, as he does, for example, to the two disciples in Emmaus.

The same idea may also be present in the story of two other figures at the beginning of Luke's gospel, Simeon and Anna. Both devout Jews of great age, they have waited a lifetime without a glimpse of their long-awaited Messiah before, at long last, God chooses to reveal Jesus to them, through his own sovereign act. Simeon knows nothing of any distinctive Christian doctrines, and yet is still 'moved by the Spirit' (Luke 2.27). Anna has never heard the 'great commission' or the 'four spiritual laws', and yet she becomes one of the first evangelists for Jesus (2.38).

This hint in these stories that the Jews might, after an extended wait, relent and accept Jesus as their Messiah may also explain why Luke devotes such a large section in Acts to reporting Stephen's speech to the Sanhedrin, one of the longest recorded sermons in the Bible. Far from being an unrelated diversion from the main storyline in Acts, the speech is absolutely critical to the central point that Luke wants to drive home. As Stephen makes clear, the great leaders in Israel's past often had to endure prolonged periods of waiting, before opposition finally turned into recognition and acceptance.

In his defence, Stephen gives pride of place to Moses, who, like Jesus, was initially rejected as a deliverer of his people, and spent years in exile before finally being accepted as their leader. Stephen also mentions Joshua, whose testimony is initially spurned but who eventually becomes the leader of Israel (compare Num. 14.6-10 with Deut. 34.9), and David, who, though chosen and anointed by Samuel, was confined for many years to commanding a band of renegades - those in distress, debt and discontented - before finally winning universal acclaim as Israel's king (1 Sam. 22.2; 2 Sam. 5.1-5).

Perhaps the most interesting figure Stephen describes as a model for Jesus, however, is Joseph. This helps to underline the fascinating parallels with the gospels in the early part of Joseph's life. Deeply and uniquely loved by his father, he is blessed with prodigious spiritual gifts from a young age. However, his vision of his brothers bowing before him incites them to bitter jealousy. Their pointed question in in Genesis 37.8, 'Do you intend to reign over us?', might well remind us of the disgruntled compatriots in Luke's parable of the ten minas who complain, 'We don't want this man to be our king' (19.14).

The similarities with Jesus increase with the events that follow. When Joseph is sent out on a mission by his father to reach his brothers, they conspire to kill him. Though one or two speak up in his defence, they are easily outnumbered. He is stripped of his beautiful robe, cast into a waterless pit where he must experience terrible thirst, and sold to Midianites for twenty pieces of silver. All of these elements find clear echoes in the New Testament.

From our perspective today, the second part of the story also has intriguing parallels with the changing fortunes of Christianity over history. Having been rejected by his own flesh and blood, Joseph rises to a position of some success in the Gentile world, but is then falsely accused and languishes in prison for a considerable time. Later the situation changes dramatically and he rises to the highest position of power, with all the levers of state at his disposal. A period of plenty follows in a Western Gentile land, where his Jewish origins are all but forgotten (like those of Esther, who initially disguises her Jewish identity for 'such a time as this').[4]

The climax of the story surely hits home today. It comes during a period of crisis and environmental catastrophe when the crop fails. At this point his long-lost brothers come back seeking assistance, but don't realise who he is. With a dramatic irony much like that accompanying the 'mysterious stranger' on the road to Emmaus, the suspense caused by their failure to recognise him makes the dramatic moment of revelation all the more telling. In the Joseph story this takes place two years into a seven-year period of famine and tribulation (45.3-11). There is great weeping and embracing. The entire Jewish nation-to-be is saved from impending extinction. It is only at this point that they, too, are exalted to a position of great favour in the Gentile land, and the Egyptians recognise and understand Joseph's Jewish origins.

Despite the long and tortuous journey that Joseph had to undergo to reach this point, he is clear about God's redemptive work through the whole situation. In Genesis 45.7 he declares that 'God sent me ahead of you to preserve for you a remnant on earth'. Later he adds, 'You meant evil against me, but God meant it for good' (50.20 ESV). What appears to be an unmitigated disaster actually conceals

God's hand in a surprising and remarkable way. The very rejection and scheming of his brothers proves ironically to result in the salvation, not only of their own lives, but of what Genesis 41.57 describes as the whole world as well.

What comes across clearly in Stephen's condensed account to the Sanhedrin is that the brothers only recognise Joseph on their *second* meeting with him in Egypt (Acts 7.13), and the experience of Moses is similar (7.35). A parallel can be traced in the story of Jephthah, the son of a harlot (as Jesus himself is described in the Talmud), who takes refuge in a distant land, having been thrown out by his brothers, only being invited back later as their deliverer (Judges 11.1-11). It seems that God in his wisdom so often saves the best until last, and while the Old Testament does not clearly teach a departing and returning Messiah, whose comeback marks a decisive moment for Israel itself, hints of such an outcome do seem occasionally to linger below the surface (see, for example, Hosea 5.15-6.3).

It may be, then, that the Joseph story provides not only a rare prophetic glimpse in the Old Testament into the Church Age up to our own day, but a portent of a future Jewish recognition of their Messiah. The experiences of Joseph's initial sojourn in Egypt find an echo in the persecution experienced by the body of Christ before its elevation by Constantine and his successors to the highest position of Gentile power, a far distance from its original Jewish identity. Likewise the weeping and repentance on the part of Joseph's brothers provides a striking foreshadowing of the future Jewish national repentance predicted in Zechariah 12:

'And I will pour out on the house of David and the inhabitants of Jerusalem a spirit of grace and supplication. They will look on me, the one they have pierced, and they will mourn for him as one mourns for an only child, and grieve bitterly for him as one grieves for a firstborn son. On that day the weeping in Jerusalem will be as great as the weeping of Hadad Rimmon in the plain of Megiddo. The land will mourn, each clan by itself, with their wives by themselves: the clan of the house of David and their wives, the clan of the house of Nathan and their wives, the clan of the house of Levi and their wives, the clan of Shimei and their wives, and all the rest of the clans and their wives.' (12.10-14)

The consequences are immediate:

'On that day a fountain will be opened to the house of David and the inhabitants of Jerusalem, to cleanse them from sin and impurity. On that day, I will banish the names of the idols from the land, and they will be remembered no more,' declares the LORD Almighty. (13.1-2).

Similar passages abound in many of the other prophetic books. Repentance will touch the whole nation and transform it. Israel will be given a new heart and a new spirit (Ezek. 36.26). For this reason Paul can say so confidently in Romans 11.26 that '*all* Israel will be saved'. Until this time, the church that he describes in Ephesians as a single body of Jews and Gentiles worshipping Christ together is still incomplete. Then, and only then, can his vision of 'one new humanity' be fully realised.

All the broken family stories in Genesis that might have implications for Israel and the church seem to have relatively happy endings. Esau runs to meet Jacob on the road. Rachel and Leah are eventually united and speak in one voice. Joseph and his brothers are ultimately reconciled.

Will it be the same for Israel and the church? Will God indeed 'turn the hearts of the parents to their children, and the hearts of the children to their parents' (Mal. 4.6)? Is the church ready for such a moment?

One thing is crystal clear: one day the Jews will finally recognise their Messiah, who *came* as a Jew, *stands now* in heaven as a Jew and who will *return* as a Jew. If this proves to be a surprising revelation for the Jewish people, it may prove to be an even greater surprise still for the church. We had better be ready!

There remains, however, one lurking shadow. When we re-read Zechariah 12 more fully, we discover that this momentous discovery by the Jewish people of their Messiah will not take place in circumstances that are at all easy or comfortable. Rather, such an event will be birthed in the wake of great conflict, involving many nations of the earth turning against Israel.

Is such a conflict inevitable? What is its background, and where will it lead? Can it throw light on the events we see taking place in the world around us today?

In order to consider this, we need to change direction. Up to now our spotlight has been upon the relationship between Judaism and Christianity. But there is an unpredictable third player of great importance for the destiny of the Jewish people in their present situation.

Surrounding the modern nation of Israel on all sides lies the world of Islam. This volatile relationship between the descendants of Abraham's two sons impacts the nature of the world we live in today, and generates uncertainty and confusion across the West. In the last two chapters we will explore the roots of this tense standoff which now exists in the Middle East.

# 11 ISRAEL AND ISHMAEL

In November 1946 a young Bedouin shepherd named Muhammed edh-Dhib stumbled and fell into a cave near the Dead Sea. What he encountered there was extraordinary. Inside was a treasure trove of Jewish scrolls going back over two thousand years, miraculously preserved by the dry conditions in the cave. Among them was a manuscript of Isaiah dating back 1100 years before the earliest known Hebrew text of the book, the Leningrad Codex.

Little did many people know that an important text in that scroll was about to reach its fulfilment:

Before she goes into labour,
   she gives birth;
before the pains come upon her,
   she delivers a son.

Who has ever heard of such things?
   Who has ever seen things like this?
Can a country be born in a day
   or a nation be brought forth in a moment?
Yet no sooner is Zion in labour
   than she gives birth to her children.   (Is. 66.7-8)

Less than two years later, the modern state of Israel came into being within a single day, just as the prophecy indicated. The discovery of the long-lost scroll proved to be a remarkable portent of the way that God was to resurrect a nation and a language that had been dormant for almost two millennia.

If the last defenders of the Jewish national dream went down fighting to the bitter end against the Romans at Masada in AD 73 (again at the Dead Sea), we should be little surprised that the re-emergence of modern-day Israel was also marred by severe conflict. When David ben Gurion proclaimed the new state of Israel on 15$^{th}$ May 1948, five Arab armies from surrounding countries immediately invaded. The Jordanians captured east Jerusalem and much of Judea and Samaria, expelling or killing Jews in the territory they took. They then annexed it, naming it 'the West Bank of Jordan'. The Jordanian claim to sovereignty was not recognized by any nation in the world apart from Britain, Iraq and the newly-created Pakistan. Only in 1967 did Israel move into these territories, an act that has caused bitter controversy ever since.

The re-establishment of Israel as a state has brought a configuration of regional tensions not dissimilar to those which existed in Old Testament times. This coalition of hostile forces surrounding ancient Israel is memorably summed up in Psalm 83:

With cunning they conspire against your people;
   they plot against those you cherish.
"Come," they say, "let us destroy them as a nation,
   so that Israel's name is remembered no more."

With one mind they plot together;
   they form an alliance against you—
the tents of Edom and the Ishmaelites,
   of Moab and the Hagrites,
Byblos, Ammon and Amalek,
   Philistia, with the people of Tyre.
Even Assyria has joined them
   to reinforce Lot's descendants. (vv. 3-8)

It cannot escape our attention that most of the modern equivalents to the peoples mentioned in the Psalm are Islamic countries or regions. The mention of 'Ishmaelites' reminds us that Muslims trace their ancestry back to Abraham's eldest son, whom they consider to have inherited the promises which the Bible attributes to Isaac. And the declared intention to destroy Israel in the Psalm is echoed today both in the charter of Hamas, and in a previously stated aim of the government of Iran.[1]

In the last chapter we touched on the repeated promises by God in the Old Testament to pour out his Spirit on Israel. There is an interesting background to these passages. Most of the times such a national reawakening is mentioned, it is in the context of a military attack on Israel by a coalition of hostile forces, against which God decisively intervenes and brings miraculous deliverance (see especially Jeremiah 30.5-8, Joel 3.9-17 and Zechariah chapters 12 and 14).

A particularly detailed account of such a scenario appears in chapters 38 and 39 of Ezekiel. The passage predicts an alliance of eight nations led by a ruler named Gog, comprising Magog, Meshek, Tubal, Persia, Cush, Put, Gomer, and Beth Togarmah. If we translate these lands into today's terms, we can identify Persia, Cush and Put with the modern states of Iran, Sudan and Libya, while the others appear to correspond to places in, or close to, modern Turkey: in other words, a group of peoples that are now Muslim nations. (Some commentators would also add Russia to this configuration as representing the 'uttermost parts of the north' - [38.6 ESV]).

In addition to reappearing in Revelation 20.8, Gog and Magog also re-emerge in the Qur'an as Yajuj and Majuj (18.96; 21.96). According to Islamic teaching, these were peoples that were spreading corruption through the earth during the time of Abraham. The Muslim scholar Ibn Kathir (1300-1373) states that 'Gog and Magog are two groups of Turks, descended from Yafith (Japheth), the father of the Turks, one of the sons of Noah.'[2]

Ezekiel's account tells us that the battle goes disastrously wrong for the enemies of Israel. Not only do the participants start fighting each other (not so unlikely, given that such a coalition today would be made up of an unstable combination of Sunni and Shi'a Muslims) but a decisive intervention by God then follows, causing a wholescale destruction of the invading forces. It is this which causes

Israel to turn back to God (39.22), leading to an outpouring of the Spirit upon the nation (39.29).

While the coming of Islam was still a very long way ahead in the future when Ezekiel received his prophecy, there is no necessary reason to suppose that the spiritual principalities attempting to control events have changed. If the demonic 'king of Persia' was battling against God's people in Daniel's time (Dan. 10.13) we should not be surprised to see threats towards Israel emerging from the same region in our own day.

But we cannot ignore the fact that Islam is now the main vehicle through which this opposition is channelled, however close or otherwise this might be to the actual message of the Qur'an (which, of course, is a matter of debate). Whatever conclusion we draw, scarcely a day goes by without us seeing this conflict being played out on a global scale.

What is it about Judaism and Islam that appears to lock them against each other as such mortal enemies? Superficially both faiths appear to have many beliefs and practices in common: an unshaken belief in the indivisible oneness of God, a common descent from Abraham, a pattern of feasts and commemorations based on a lunar calendar, a code of strict dietary and hygiene laws, the custom of circumcision, times for regular daily prayer, and so on. In some areas, such as ritual purity, slaughter of animals and the traditions of death and burial, the correspondences are particularly striking.[3] In addition,

Arabic and Hebrew are closely related languages and include many similar words.

The Qur'an also shares many stories in common with the Old Testament: Adam, Noah, Abraham, Joseph, Moses and David and a host of other Biblical characters all appear prominently. Not all the details are the same, and some are given a different theological 'twist' because of a different understanding of sin and the mercy of God. On the one hand, for example, Adam is forgiven for eating the forbidden fruit in the Garden of Eden with no ongoing consequence for the human race, and yet on the other Abraham is commanded by God not to ask for mercy on the inhabitants of Sodom but to leave them to their fate (Sura 11.76). There is, however, despite such discrepancies, a great deal of common ground.

There are even traces of later Jewish Rabbinical teaching which appear to have found their way into the Qur'an. One statement, that 'whoever kills a person is as if he has killed the whole of humankind, and whoever saves the life of a person is as if he has saved the life of the whole of humankind' (5.31) is almost identical to another found over a century earlier in the Jerusalem Talmud (Sanhedrin 4.5).

Many of these influences came directly from Jews living in Arabia in the time of Muhammad. During much of the earlier part of his life, he seems to have been quite open to dialogue with Jews and Christians. He initially directed his followers to pray towards Jerusalem and confirmed the validity of their sacred books, even at one point advocating the recitation of the Torah (Sura 3.93):

> We believe in Allah, and in what has been revealed to us, and in what has been revealed to Abraham, Ishmael, Isaac, Jacob and his children, and in what has been given to Moses and Jesus and what has been given to the prophets from their Lord: We make no difference between any of them, and to Him we submit ourselves. (2.136)

Moreover, he repeatedly affirms the special calling on the Jewish people, in passages such as the following:

> We gave the children of Israel the book and the wisdom and the prophethood, and provided them with good things, and preferred them above all (people of) the world (45.16)

> O children of Israel! call to mind the (special) favour which I bestowed upon you, and that I preferred you to all others (for My Message). (2.47; similarly 2.122)[4]

Even in the later revelations, this view appears to remain unchanged:

> Recall when Moses said to his people, "O my people, remember the blessing of Allah upon you when He made prophets from among you, made you kings and gave you what He did not give to anyone in the worlds." (5.20)

However, during the time that Muhammad was in Mecca, and saw the Jews and Christians were unwilling to accept his message, he began to turn against them. It was during this period that a more antagonistic spirit began to emerge in the revelations:

O you who believe, do not take the Jews and the Christians for intimate friends. (5.51)

And you will certainly find that the people most hostile against the believers are the Jews and the ones who ascribe partners to Allah. (5.82)

Fight those People of the Book who do not believe in Allah, nor in the Last Day, and do not take as unlawful what Allah and His Messenger have declared as unlawful, and do not profess the Faith of Truth; (fight them) until they pay jizyah with their own hands while they are subdued. (9.29)

More disturbing, perhaps, is a statement attributed to Muhammad in the Hadith, a collection of supplementary traditions about his life and teaching (and quoted prominently in the charter of Hamas), in which he states of the Last Day, when Jesus returns:

The Hour will not be established until you fight with the Jews, and the stone behind which a Jew will be hiding will say: 'O Muslim! There is a Jew hiding behind me, so kill him.'[5]

Despite such harsh statements, Jewish communities appeared to flourish under Islamic rule, often far better than they did in the supposedly 'Christian' West. Some rose to positions of considerable power and influence, and Arabic became the language of many Jewish scholarly works. When the Ottomans invaded Byzantium in 1493 they were welcomed by the downtrodden Jewish population, and the new ruler, Sultan Mehmet II, invited them 'to ascend the site of the Imperial Throne, to dwell in the best of the land, each beneath his Dine and his fig tree, with silver and with gold, with wealth and with cattle...'.[6] Subsequently the Ottoman Empire became a haven for many Jews fleeing persecution in Europe.

It was only moves towards the re-establishment of the state of Israel in 1948 that we see a concerted wave of hostility generated across the Muslim world towards the Jewish people. One of the first instigators, Haj Amin Al-Husseini, who had been appointed Grand Mufti in Jerusalem by the British, organised a series of pogroms and riots against the Jews in Palestine between the wars. One eye-witness to the worst of these in 1929, during which British officials stood by and did nothing, writes as follows:

For eight days the country was given over to an orgy of slaughter, rape, castration and unspeakable mutilation. The worst barbarisms took place at Hebron, Safed, Jaffa and Motza. The victims - men, women and children - were beaten, stabbed, their limbs amputated, stomachs were ripped open, and women were raped. I have met survivors, who - if they can bring themselves to speak of what happened - remember recognizing among their assailants Arab "friends" who had been regular guests in their homes. I have an album of horrifying photographs taken in hospital after the pogrom; they show the hacked bodies of the survivors, and amputated hands and fingers laid out on tables.[7]

It was largely at Al-Husseini's instigation that the Arab Revolt of 1936–39 took place, during which Arabic language leaflets decorated with the swastika were distributed. Al-Husseini later met with Hitler in 1941 to discuss the extermination of the Jews, became an associate of Himmler and Eichmann and went on to recruit Bosnian Muslims for the SS. In a broadcast on Radio Berlin in March 1944 he declared as follows:

Arabs, rise as one man and fight for your sacred rights. Kill the Jews wherever you find them. This pleases God, history, and religion. This saves your honor. God is with you.[8]

Against the background of such an unholy alliance it is not altogether surprising to see the current vogue for Holocaust denial among those opposed to the modern state of Israel. In 1983 Mahmoud Abbas, now President of the Palestinian National Authority wrote a book entitled *The Other Side: the Secret Relationship between Nazism and Zionism* which questioned whether the gas chambers were used against Jews or that six million perished. In December 2006 the Iranian Foreign Ministry hosted an international Holocaust-denial conference, which was addressed among others by French holocaust denier Robert Faurisson and former Ku Klux Klan head David Duke. In recent history an Arabic translation of Hitler's *Mein Kampf* became one of the best-selling books in Palestinian bookshops.[9] Today around a third of Israeli Arabs deny that the Holocaust ever took place.[10]

But however much the ultimate source of the hostility that flows from the Arab world towards their Jewish neighbours might appear to be triggered by the founding of the modern nation of Israel, perhaps underscored by certain passages in the Qur'an and Hadith, I would like to suggest that the real source of the problem lies back in a hasty and ill-considered decision made four thousand years ago. To explore this, we need to return once more to the pages of Genesis, and God's calling of Abraham.

Sarah knows that God has promised Abraham a son, but is also aware that she is barren and unable to have children of her own, as we saw in Chapter One. As a result, she suggests that Abraham tries having a child with her maidservant Hagar. Like all attempts to 'help God out', the result is a disaster. Discovering that Hagar loses respect for her when she becomes pregnant, Sarah begins to ill-treat her, causing Hagar to run away.

At a spring in the desert a broken Hagar encounters the angel of the Lord. The angel tells her to go back to Sarah, but promises to multiply her seed far beyond anything she can count (Gen. 16.9-10). He also instructs her to name the child Ishmael, meaning 'God hears' and tells Hagar that

> He will be a wild donkey of a man;
> his hand will be against everyone
> and everyone's hand against him,
> and he will live in hostility
> towards all his brothers." (16.12)

There are several important things to notice here. Firstly, it is *God himself* who initiates the encounter: the angel of the Lord is the one who finds Hagar, not the other way round. As I have shown elsewhere, the angel who reveals God's heart has huge parallels with the coming of Christ as portrayed by John in his gospel, being both *sent* as God's spokesman (v.11), and yet also appearing to *be* God himself (v.13).[11]

Secondly, though God recognises her pain, he still tells her to submit to Sarah, however unjust this might seem in human terms. The blessing that follows comes only *after* the instruction to submit.

Thirdly, the blessing on her child-to-be is very similar to that given to Isaac (26.24) who later lives by this very same well (24.62). We should note, then, that the Arabs, Hagar's descendants, are the only people in existence today apart from the Jews to be ordained by a direct promise of God (16.10; 17.20; 21.18). Yet this promise has a sting in its tail: it is to be accompanied by hostility to all those around, and towards Ishmael's kinsmen specifically.

Finally we should note that without God's direct intervention, Hagar is lost. It is only *after* the angel reveals himself to her that she is able to experience a personal relationship with God ('I have now seen the One who sees me', v.13).

All these points, I believe, have huge relevance to the Muslim world today, and the way in which God is beginning to move among them. But the story of Hagar and her son also has relevance for the violent events that we see daily on our television screens. History has an extraordinary propensity to recycle old wounds.

Although Hagar returns to Sarah, the tension between them comes to the fore again after the miraculous birth of Isaac, the supernatural answer to God's promise. This time it is Sarah, with Abraham's reluctant consent, who pushes for Hagar to be sent into exile. It must have come as a catastrophic blow: one can only imagine the pain and anger going through Hagar's mind at being forced out into the unknown.

It is even harder for her now abandoned son, who has grown up as Abraham's presumptive heir. At the root of Ishmael's anguish is a sense of rejection, a father wound, a need to prove himself. Perhaps at the back of his mind is the forlorn hope that he will somehow earn his way back into his father's favour. We should remember the parallel with his maternal ancestor Ham, who also experienced his father's rejection (Gen. 9.22-25).

But hope is running out. Hagar only has a limited supply of water, and when that runs dry, only death beckons. She sits down under a bush and they both begin to sob. God hears promises to make Ishmael into a great nation. Then he opens her eyes and she sees a well of water whose existence she had not known about before.

I believe this passage speaks prophetically to our own day. In the Bible wells are used as a picture of salvation (Gen. 16.13-14; Is. 12.3; John 4.6-10). Although Muslims are today in a dry place spiritually, trying to win the favour of a God who appears remote and inaccessible, just as Abraham was for Ishmael, and who can never be called 'Father' (a title not given to Allah in the Qur'an), he is hearing their cry and opening their eyes to redemption. Jesus is revealing himself to individuals through dreams and visions on a daily basis. Consequently, more Muslims have come to Christ in the last thirty years than for an entire millennium.

It is important to recognise that God remained with Ishmael as he grew up in the desert (21.20), even though he was cut off from his family roots. He went on, like his later nephew Jacob, to have twelve sons who become twelve tribes, who settled in Havilah, almost certainly modern-day Arabia, and 'lived in hostility toward all the tribes related to them' (Gen. 25.18).

Many Arabs trace their lineage back to Kedar, Ishmael's second son, from whom the Muslim scholar Hisham Ibn Muhammad al-Kalbi (737–819) established a direct family lineage down to Mohammad himself. In Ezekiel 27.21 Arabia and the 'princes of Kedar' appear together, underlining their close association. Reaching the height of its power in the 6th century BC, the Kedarites were wealthy through trade and controlled much of the Arabian peninsula. Their skill in archery was one that Ishmael himself had gained in the desert (Gen. 21.20; Is. 21.17).

After 2 Samuel the name Ishmael disappears from view, but 'Arab' begins to appear in its place. The Arabs are mentioned initially as bringing tribute to Israel (1 Kings 10.15; 2 Chronicles 9.14 and 17.11), as standing in opposition to Israel (2 Chronicles 22.1, 26.7; Nehemiah 2.19, 4.7, 6.1) and as reaping judgement on that account (Is. 21.13-17; Jer. 25.24).

The same is true of references to Kedar: its people bring tribute to Israel (Is. 60.7), stand in opposition to God's people (Ps. 120.5-6) and suffer judgement as a result (Is. 21.16-17; Jer. 49.28-29). Yet there is also a promise a something much better for them on the horizon:

Let the wilderness and its towns raise their voices;
 let the settlements where Kedar lives rejoice.     (Is 42.11)

Significantly, this passage occurs in the context of God's commission to his 'servant' (42.1) which describes both Israel itself (42.19; 43.10; 49.3) and more specifically its Messiah (49.5; 52.13-15) to be 'a light for the Gentiles, to open eyes that are blind, to free captives from prison and to release from the dungeon those who sit in darkness' (Is. 42.6-7).

In the New Testament the three references to Arabs and Arabia also produce a range of varying associations. In one instance Paul mentions Arabia as the location of Mount Sinai (Gal 4.25), which he sees as representing an old covenant based on law, in contrast to the heavenly Jerusalem which portrays the new covenant based on faith. Here Arabia provides a setting for dryness, hopelessness and rule-bound religion, and although Paul is here attacking Jewish legalism, the reference to Hagar, the mother of Ishmael, is striking.

In another instance Arabia appears as the place where Paul took refuge for an extended period after his conversion, just as Jesus who was driven into the wilderness after his baptism (Gal. 1.17). In this case Arabia becomes a setting for reflection, revelation and encounter, as well as great challenge and inner wrestling. Many Muslims who come to faith in Christ through a direct revelation, as Paul did, have to go through a similar period of wrestling, as they come to terms with a triune God very different from the one in the Qur'an, a God whose justice and mercy can only be reconciled through the death of Jesus.

Finally we should note that Arabs take the last place in the list of those present at Pentecost. Encountering the good news for the first time, they are cut to the heart and return to their home country filled with the Spirit and exalting the name of Jesus. Here is a picture of salvation and new life.

The root of the word 'Arab' also appears in the Hebrew name 'Arabah', the designation in the Old Testament for the rift valley following the course of the River Jordan. Today this marks the east side of the state of Israel on its post-1967 boundaries, establishing the frontier which divides it from its Arab neighbours. Geologically the valley is created by the division between the Arabian plate and the African plate, which are inexorably moving apart from one another. In some ways this is emblematic of how radical Islam seems to pull further and further apart from the Judeo-Christian values of the West.

At the centre of this geological and geopolitical divide lies the Dead Sea, the very place where we began this chapter, which lies at 400 metres below sea level, the lowest point on the Earth's land surface. As the site of the ill-fated cities of Sodom and Gomorrah, and the final Zealot stronghold at Masada, it is in some ways a symbol of man's rebellion against God and the inevitable judgement that ensues. Having no outlet into the ocean, it only ever receives, but never gives.

As a result it has one of the highest concentrations of salt of any body of water on the earth, being almost ten times more salty than the oceans. These conditions make it impossible for living things to exist in its waters. Like dead religion, it looks refreshing, but is actually devoid of life.

Yet in chapter 47 of Ezekiel we see an extraordinary picture. Water is flowing out from the south side of the altar of the temple in Jerusalem towards the Dead Sea. As the water travels eastwards, it increases from a small stream to become a mighty torrent.

There is a striking account of Ezekiel trying to cross this river. At first he goes in up to his ankles, then he progresses up to his knees, before finally the water reaches up to his waist. At this point he is unable to wade through any further and has to return to the bank. He recognises that the river is too wide for anyone to be able to cross.

We might see in Ezekiel's failed attempt to reach the other side a picture of the futility of all religious systems. They are attempting to cross the unbridgeable gulf between man and God by their own efforts.

No system of rules, whether in Islam, Judaism, or traditional forms of Christianity, can ever bring us to our true destiny. We are, in a sense, trying to keep our feet firmly on the ground and as a result remain anchored to the riverbed. The only solution is to surrender our own strength completely and allow the water to carry us. It has to be the work of Christ alone, to which we can add nothing.

However when these waters reach the Arabah and enter the Dead Sea, something remarkable happens. The waters of the sea become fresh again so that they can support a vast quantity of fish. I believe that this is in part an extraordinary picture of how God will one day use the Jews to touch the Islamic world with the good news about Jesus.

The same supernatural water-source is mentioned again in Zechariah 13.1. The context is the same as the passage in

Ezekiel that we considered earlier in the chapter: the nations have gathered around Jerusalem to destroy it, but are defeated through the direct intervention of God himself. After pouring out 'a spirit of grace and supplication', causing Israel to mourn for the Lord that they have rejected and nailed to the cross, like the loss of a firstborn son (12.10), the fountain is described as going both westwards and eastwards from Jerusalem, to the Mediterranean as well as the Dead Sea (14.8).

There is only one conclusion that can be drawn from this: the life flowing into the Islamic world, as well as into the West, *will be the direct consequence of Israel's coming to faith in Jesus.* A clue to this can be found in Christ's own statement in the temple in John 7.38:

Whoever *believes in me*, as Scripture has said, rivers of living water will flow from within them.

We can search the scriptures from Genesis to Malachi and find no exact reference to the words Jesus uses here, and there seems to be no clear alternative to the view that he is referring to Ezekiel's river. It is *Israel's belief in Christ* that will cause the river to flow.

This is the end the church needs to pray for, having done everything in its power to prevent from happening for most of its history. The order of events at the end of Zechariah, as well as Christ's own statement in Matthew 23.39 and the implication of Paul's remark in Romans 11.25-26 seems to make it clear that Jesus *will not* return until the nation of Israel has accepted him *en masse*. Only then can this ancient feud in Genesis, which now scars the whole world and leaves many of all nations living in fear and trepidation, be brought to its final, glorious resolution.

From our perspective today, however, this still seems a long way off. The modern state of Israel appears to be mired in a battle for her very existence and has become an obstacle to peace in the eyes of many in the world. In the final chapter we will consider the challenges she faces and, in particular, the rightful ownership of the land on which she sits.

# 12 WHOSE LAND?

As we saw in the last chapter, the land of Israel covers one of the most hotly-contended swathes of real-estate on the planet. In Ezekiel 5.5, God says that it is 'set in the centre of the nations, with countries all around her'. In Lamentations 1.17 we read the following:

The LORD has decreed for Jacob
 that his neighbours become his foes;
Jerusalem has become
 an unclean thing among them.

Clearly little has changed over thousands of years. Conflict over competing claims on its limited resources was nothing new: as early as Genesis 13, we find Abraham's herdsmen arguing with those of Lot over the allocation of land. Thirteen chapters later conflict resurfaces again, this time between Isaac's herdsmen and the Philistines over the ownership of wells, and the issue of water supply remains a key flashpoint between Israel and the Palestinians even today.

By the time of Nehemiah, one of the last books of Old Testament history, the legacy of hostility had carried on unabated over many centuries, and the presence of Jews within the land was still stirring up strife and resentment among the local inhabitants. In Nehemiah 4.7-8 what we might describe in today's language as an alliance of Palestinians, Arabs, Samaritans and Jordanians were conspiring together against the Jewish occupation and fortification of Jerusalem.

In this sense we are in a similar situation today. Thousands of years on, the same issues keep coming back and we are no nearer to finding an answer. For this reason, I enter the barrage of claim and counter-claim about ownership with a certain amount of trepidation, accepting that many readers may feel that I am being glib and superficial in the observations I am about to make. The last thing that I want to do is to cause offence on such a volatile and emotive issue. But it is not a subject we can easily avoid in the context of all that we have shared so far.

There are two things I want to make clear from the outset. Firstly, I have the greatest respect for those who hold opposite opinions in these matters, who are often motivated by a strong sense of compassion, integrity and a righteous anger against all forms of oppression and injustice. Like them, I recognize that skewed theological judgements can result in disastrous consequences at a human level when outworked in the realm of politics on a national or international scale.

Secondly, however, I should point out that where the case against the modern nation of Israel becomes entangled with 'replacement theology', as it so often does, it is doomed to fail. Israel's right to exist in her historic homeland within secure boundaries, to defend herself from attack and to exercise undivided sovereignty over Jerusalem cannot stand purely on the basis of natural justice (because in this the Palestinians can put forward a very strong case of their own), or on the dictates of international bodies (which, however well-meaning, rest ultimately on human foundations). Ultimately the right and wrong behind these questions stand or fall on the revealed will of God, as demonstrated in the Bible. And if so, that brings us to the billion-dollar question: to whom do these territories really belong?

The simple answer, of course, is that the land is the property of God himself. In Leviticus 25.23 God reminds Israel that 'the land is mine and you reside in my land as foreigners and strangers'. In Joshua 5.13-14 the angelic commander of God's army informs Joshua that he is completely even-handed, being neither on the side of Israel or its enemies. And there are plenty of verses in scripture to remind us that God has no favourites (Deut. 10.17; 2 Chron. 19.7; Mark 12.14; Rom. 2.11; Col. 3.25).

If this were all the Bible had to say on the subject, the question would be a relatively simple one to resolve. But as I have already said, we are not dealing purely with natural justice here, but with the direct promises of God. And these are very clear.

## 1. The Bible clearly promises the land to Israel

In Genesis Chapter 15 God makes a solemn covenant with Abraham in which he declares:

'To your descendants I give this land, from the Wadi of Egypt to the great river, the Euphrates – the land of the Kenites, Kenizzites, Kadmonites, Hittites, Perizzites, Rephaites, Amorites, Canaanites, Girgashites and Jebusites.' (vv. 18-21)

If there should be any doubt as to *which* descendants of Abraham are to reap this blessing, verse 13 makes it abundantly clear that it is the Jews themselves:

'Know for certain that for four hundred years your descendants will be strangers in a country not their own and that they will be enslaved and ill-treated there.'

Moreover, this was no ordinary covenant. As we pointed out in Chapter Three, it was normal at this time for both parties to an agreement to walk between the divided carcasses of sacrificed animals to act out the awful consequences that would fall on either side should the terms of the covenant be broken. Yet it is striking here that it is only God himself, in the form of a smoking brazier and a blazing torch, who does this, suggesting that *he alone* would bear the punishment should Abraham or his descendants break the terms of the covenant.

Nowhere does the New Testament teach that this covenant has been suspended through the coming of Christ. Both Mary and Zechariah affirm the promises made to Abraham and his descendants (Luke 1.55, 73) and Jesus himself hints at the continuing validity of such decrees (Matt. 5.18). Stephen in turn acknowledges the gift of the land in his speech to the Sanhedrin in Acts 7.5, and Paul, while seeing Christ himself ultimately receiving the promised inheritance, clearly underlines the unconditional nature of the promise made (Gal. 3.16-18). To the Romans he points out that 'God's gifts and his call are irrevocable' (Rom. 11.29), a statement which while not *specifically* referring to the land, cannot *exclude* it.

Any lingering doubts about the matter should be cleared up by Psalm 105, which declares:

He remembers his covenant for ever,
    the promise he made, for a thousand generations,
the covenant he made with Abraham,
    the oath he swore to Isaac.
He confirmed it to Jacob as a decree,
    to Israel as an *everlasting covenant*:
'To you I will give the land of Canaan
    as the portion you will inherit.' (vv. 8-11)

While we might speculate on the length of 'a thousand generations', expressions such as 'for ever' and 'everlasting' are pretty clear. The land has been promised to Israel as an eternal possession.

Rather surprisingly, the Qur'an seems to back the Bible up on this point. Sura 5.20 declares that:

> O my people, enter the Holy Land which Allah has
> destined for you, and do not turn back, lest you should
> turn losers.

Sura 10.93 declares similarly that

> We settled the Children of Israel in a beautiful dwelling-
> place, and provided for them sustenance of the best.[1]

Although the existence of the modern state of Israel has
caused great anger and resentment to Muslims across the
world, it has not been universal: the late King Faysal of
Iraq, for example, openly expressed his sympathy for the
Zionist movement, while the King of Bahrain has recently
spoken up in defence of Israel.[2]

## 2. The Bible clearly foretells the regathering of the Jews to their homeland

The great Victorian preacher Charles Spurgeon once said,
'I think we do not attach sufficient importance to the
restoration of the Jews. We do not think enough of it. But
certainly, if there is anything promised in the Bible, it is
this.'[3]

Spurgeon's confidence in this matter, almost a century
before the foundation of the modern state of Israel, was
shared by a number of influential Victorian evangelicals (as
we saw in Chapter Ten) whose standpoint may ultimately
have contributed to a climate which produced the Balfour
Declaration, later described by Winston Churchill as a
'solemn obligation .... to that unhappy mass of scattered,

persecuted, wandering Jews whose intense, unchanging, unconquerable desire has been for a National Home'.[4]

Behind such a firmly rooted belief lay a number of clear Old Testament predictions of a final return of the Jews to their homeland. Amos 9, for instance, declares that:

'The days are coming,' declares the LORD,

'when the reaper will be overtaken by the ploughman
    and the planter by the one treading grapes.
New wine will drip from the mountains
    and flow from all the hills,
and I will bring my people Israel back from exile.

'They will rebuild the ruined cities and live in them.
    They will plant vineyards and drink their wine;
    they will make gardens and eat their fruit.
I will plant Israel in their own land,
    never again to be uprooted
    from the land I have given them,'

says the LORD your God. (vv. 13-15)

Returns from exile have taken place before, of course. What is different in this passage is that it has to refer to the *last* one: careful reading of the final verse will show that it cannot be referring to Babylonian captivity.

The same can be said of the final return described in Ezekiel 39, which takes place after the as yet unfought battle which we described in the last chapter, and precedes the outpouring of God's spirit on the nation:

'When I have brought them back from the nations and have gathered them from the countries of their enemies, I will be proved holy through them in the sight of many nations. Then they will know that I am the LORD their God, for though I sent them into exile among the nations, I will gather them to their own land, not leaving any behind. I will no longer hide my face from them, for I will pour out my Spirit on the people of Israel, declares the Sovereign LORD.' (vv. 27-29)

Similarly, Isaiah 11.11 says:

In that day the Lord will reach out his hand a second time to reclaim the surviving remnant of his people from Assyria, from Lower Egypt, from Upper Egypt, from Cush, from Elam, from Babylonia, from Hamath and from the islands of the Mediterranean.

The fact that this prophecy is followed by signs that remain unfulfilled to this day (vv. 15-16) shows once more that it cannot have been fulfilled at a previous time in history.

Furthermore, in Luke 21.20-24 Jesus describes a scattering of Jews to take place *after his death*, but with a hint that this would end with a restoration of Jerusalem to Jewish control:

'When you see Jerusalem being surrounded by armies, you will know that its desolation is near. Then let those who are in Judea flee to the mountains, let those in the city get out, and let those in the country not enter the city. For this is the time of punishment *in fulfilment of all that has been written.* How dreadful it will be in those days for pregnant women and nursing mothers! There will be great distress in the land and wrath against this people. *They will fall by the sword and will be taken as prisoners to all the nations.* Jerusalem will be trampled on by the Gentiles *until the times of the Gentiles are fulfilled.*'

Could Jesus be speaking about a time that is still a living memory for some readers, when Israel gained control of the entire city of Jerusalem in 1967? If so, we can interpret this as a telling indication that prophecy is still being fulfilled in our own times. Reading the passage again with the verses that follow makes it abundantly clear that Jesus *specifically* linked his return to this restoration of Jewish sovereignty over Jerusalem. In doing so he was simply reaffirming the promises given in Isaiah 11 and Jeremiah 23 where a restored, regathered Israel is directly associated with the inauguration of the Messiah's rule.

It is noteworthy, however, that these promises to regather the nation are not vouchsafed on the faithfulness or unfaithfulness of the Jews themselves, but on the reputation of God's own name, which will be a witness to all nations:

'Therefore say to the Israelites, "This is what the Sovereign LORD says: *it is not for your sake*, people of Israel, that I am going to do these things, but *for the sake of my holy name*, which you have profaned among the nations where you have gone. I will show the holiness of my great name, which has been profaned among the nations, the name you have profaned among them. *Then the nations will know that I am the LORD*, declares the Sovereign LORD, *when I am proved holy through you* before their eyes.

'"For I will take you out of the nations; *I will gather you from all the countries* and bring you back into *your own land*."' (Ezek. 36.22-24)

If it is God himself who is ultimately causing these events to take place, we should be less hasty in rushing to human judgements. By restoring a long-lost nation to its historic roots, he is first and foremost vindicating his own name. Ancient promises are being fulfilled in our own time.

And it is not just the Bible that declares that these things will come to pass. Once more, it is perhaps surprising to see the same assurances of a regathered Israel in the last days appear in the Qur'an:

And We said unto the Children of Israel after him: Dwell in the land; but when the promise of the Hereafter cometh to pass We shall bring you as a crowd gathered out of various nations. (Qur'an 17.104)

## 3. There is a need for repentance on both sides of the divide

No-one can deny the trauma and heartbreak the Palestinians have suffered as a people who feel themselves to be stateless and powerless. Some 700,000 who fled their homes 1948 were never able to return, although there were also large-scale expulsions of Jews from Arab lands in consequence. Appalling massacres, such as that Deir Yassin in April 1948 in which 150 bodies, some heavily mutilated, were thrown into a cistern by the Jewish militia Irgun,[5] or the Sabra and Shabra massacres in Lebanon in 1982, carried out by so-called 'Christian' Phalangists with the apparent assent of the Israeli Defence Force, are sharply etched on Palestinian consciousness. In more recent times the separation barrier and the security checks deemed necessary by Israel to defend itself are deemed by most Palestinian Arabs as oppressive, humiliating and discriminatory, while continued expansion of Jewish settlements outside the pre-1967 borders is seen as provocative in the extreme and creates real anger and resentment.

Israel has also been much attacked on the ethics of its operations against Hamas. The Old Testament clearly teaches balanced, proportionate retribution as opposed to the disproportionate retribution of Lamech (Gen. 4.24). Clearly there have been tragic abuses, though Western media have often been less than even-handed in their coverage of the conflict.[6]

It has to be said, however, that countries with appalling human rights records seem to be first in line to accuse Israel. In fact, Commander Richard Kemp, former commander of British forces in Afghanistan, points out that the Israeli Defence Forces have done 'more to safeguard the rights of civilians in a combat zone than any other army in the history of warfare' and that it did so 'while facing an enemy that deliberately positioned its military capability behind the human shield of the civilian population'.

He points out that, during Operation Cast Lead in December 2008-January 2009, for which Israel was heavily criticised for its military tactics,

the IDF took extraordinary measures to give Gaza civilians notice of targeted areas, dropping over 2 million leaflets, and making over 100,000 phone calls. Many missions that could have taken out Hamas military capability were aborted to prevent civilian casualties. During the conflict, the IDF allowed huge amounts of humanitarian aid into Gaza. To deliver aid virtually into your enemy's hands is, to the military tactician, normally quite unthinkable. But the IDF took on those risks.[7]

It is not my intention, however, to whitewash the state of Israel, but simply to point out that the dynamics of the situation are a great deal more complex than the news media often portray. Undoubtedly grave mistakes have been made, and while Israel may have achieved a temporary success in some of its tactical operations, it has clearly failed to win the battle for hearts and minds in the West, let alone among the Palestinians themselves.

We must never forget, however, that despite the enormous suffering experienced by the Palestinian people, Israel is facing in Hamas an organization openly dedicated to its destruction, which openly feeds hatred towards Jews and seems to applaud and encourage random acts of violence towards innocent Israeli civilians. Pro-Israelis in Palestinian areas can be brutally treated, recalling the brutal way in which the Canaanites attacked the Gibeonites for collaborating with Israel in Joshua 10.4. One of Israel's greatest Prime Ministers, Golda Meir, once said, "Peace will come when the Arabs love their children more than they hate us."[8] Clearly there is a deficit of love and forgiveness on both sides of the divide. We need the Prince of Peace!

## 4. Natural justice only operates effectively within the boundaries of God's revealed will

Every true Christian supporter of Israel should wrestle with the hurt and trauma of the Palestinians. God's love for the Palestinian people is overwhelming, as it is for every one of us, and he hears every cry of pain and the longing for a better life, just as he heard Ishmael's cry of distress in Genesis 21.17.

Clearly, we have a responsibility to listen to both sides of the argument. We need to hear the call of despair that goes up from the Palestinian people. Yet while it is one thing (and a very noble calling indeed) to champion the cause of the Palestinians, it is quite another thing to demonise Israel in the process, or treat her as a pariah state, whatever her mistakes and short-sightedness. With their appalling record in the past, both the church and Western governments generally have forfeited all moral right to do so.

For this reason, we should be cautious in lecturing on morality and justice. A 'holier-than-thou' attitude towards Israel sits uncomfortably with centuries of persecution and cruelty towards the Jewish people. Against this background, the campaign of BDS (boycott-disinvestment-sanctions) advocated by trade unions, educational establishments and even churches against Israeli businesses and academic institutions is particularly disturbing. It carries ominous echoes for Jews of the way that so many ordinary Germans, including many Christians, participated in boycotts of Jewish shops and the dismissal of Jewish academics under the Nazis in the 1930s. Such actions led ultimately to the acceptance of, or acquiescence to, far more heinous crimes.

The danger for Christians in aligning themselves against Israel, therefore, is that they may simply be rekindling an ancient prejudice which unleashed the tragic mistakes of the past. Messianic Rabbi Dr. David Friedman has warned that 'history shows us that the Church does not stand on any high moral ground by which to tell Israelis how to act … if the Church engages in anti-Israeli action, Jesus is further driven away from his own people, compounding the historic sin of Christianity against Jewish civilization.'[9]

Likewise Canon Andrew White, no stranger to conflict resolution in the Middle East, points out that Israel is the only country in the Middle East where Christians are protected and where their numbers are increasing. He too laments the 'terrible symmetry between this animosity towards Israel and the historic Christian enmity towards the Jewish people'.[10] He goes on to draw out these parallels between historic anti-Semitism and the anti-Israel campaigns of today in particularly blunt terms:

The early Church falsely scapegoated the Jews for the death of Jesus; today's Church falsely scapegoats the State of Israel for the crimes committed against *it* by the Palestinians. The early Church demonised and dehumanised the Jews through diabolical blood libels; today's church demonises and dehumanises Israel by falsely claiming that it is wiping out the Palestinians and wantonly killing their children. The early Church was party to the slaughter of Jews in pogroms throughout Europe resulting from its incitement against the Jews as the killers of God; the modern Church is party to the genocidal attacks on Israelis, resulting from its endorsement of the Arab and Muslim narrative on Israel which incites the mass murder of Israelis and Jews throughout the world.[11]

While not all may agree with this assessment, it is important for us all to recognise how the Holocaust, and the long crescendo of historical events that led up to it, plays a central role in the shaping of Jewish national consciousness today, much as the cross does for our identity as Christians. Many of those fighting for the Palestinian cause forget that the very people they view as the 'enemy' have a collective history scarred by centuries of oppression, rejection and persecution that partly moulds this consciousness.

Israel is a country whose very identity is shaped in part by a genocide that within living memory wiped out over a third of the world's Jews. It is distressingly naïve, therefore, to expect it to make major concessions to an organisation whose stated aim is to wipe it off the map. History has shown us the disastrous consequences when attempts to rebalance injustice or inequality are driven by envy, resentment or a scapegoating of those perceived to be the 'enemy', without a real desire to understand the opposing viewpoint. Rwanda, Zimbabwe, Syria and Iraq stand out in different ways as dire warnings of the result of such blind factional strife.

Many Israelis and Jews across the world have, to their credit, attempted to reach across the divide and stand with the Palestinians in their suffering. However, all too often, when a Palestinian attempts to do the opposite, they risk facing ostracism from within their community or even death threats. The real tragedy of this is that moderate voices within the Palestinian community have been drowned out.

One sign of hope is that there are believers in Jesus on both sides of the divide. Small attempts to reach across the cultural barrier may seem insignificant now, but offer hope for transformation in the longer term. If mutual suspicions are to be broken down and genuine reconciliation achieved, it has to begin at a personal level. True reconciliation is to see God in the face of your estranged brother, as Jacob did with Esau (Gen. 33.10).

One real contribution we can make is to pray with passion and conviction. However, it is important when we pray that we are seeking God's will, not our own preconceived ideas or a political agenda driven by the news media. When our own well-intentioned and heartfelt desire for natural justice conflicts with what the Bible actually says (as, for example, with the issue of gay marriage) we need to think carefully.

Although I write as someone with a passion for the plight of the Palestinians, we should be wary of simply allowing the laws of natural justice to overturn God's revealed will. While it is every Christian's responsibility to pray fervently for the Palestinian people and God's blessing upon them, and to stand forthrightly for justice and fairness, we need to recognise that such transformation will only come as God blesses Israel herself (Gen.12.3) rather than through short-term political solutions. In the Old Testament, rulers of Israel were sometimes punished for being too lenient (1 Sam 15.9-26), as well as too harsh (1 Kings 12.12-19). Our picture of justice and equity is not the same as God's.

Jonathan Bernis writes,

Support for Israel does not mean we believe God loves Jews more than Arabs or Israelis more than Palestinians. It is simply a recognition that God, in His sovereignty, chose to give this land to the Children of Israel. It is their inheritance, regardless of their spiritual condition. That purpose has not changed; indeed, it cannot be abolished by the will or actions of men.[12]

While it is clear that there are many, many things wrong with the modern state of Israel (just as there are with our own countries), our response must take on board prophetic truths that have been spelt out abundantly clearly in scripture. Outside this revealed will of God there can be no true justice. If Zionism is simply a flawed human construct, it will inevitably collapse under the weight of its own futility. However, those who out of the deepest and most heartfelt desire to aid and bless the Palestinians seek to bring about the downfall of the Jewish nation might do well to heed the wise words of Gamaliel, as recorded by Luke in Acts:

For if their purpose or activity is of human origin, it will fail. But if it is from God, you will not be able to stop these men; *you will only find yourselves fighting against God.*' (Acts 5.38-39)

Let us not fall victim ourselves to the same kind of mistake today that he warned about almost two thousand years ago.

## 5. Can there be lasting peace before Jesus returns?

There is nothing inevitable about enmity between Israelis and Palestinians. In Genesis 20.17 Abraham prays for Abimelech and his family, the ruler of the Philistines, their distant forbears, and in 21.31-32 he makes a covenant of friendship with them. In Genesis 26.31 his son Isaac also forges a covenant of peace with the Philistines, and two verses earlier we are told that Abimelech did nothing but good to him. 1 Samuel 27 tells how David took refuge with the Philistines when he was fleeing from King Saul. When the Philistines chose to bless Israel, they in turn reaped blessing (Genesis 20.14-18).

If Palestinian leaders were truly to renounce violence and recognise God's sovereign hand in Israel, as Abimelech did with Isaac when he said, 'We saw clearly that the LORD was with you' (Gen. 26.28), the seeds of reconciliation might one day be sown. From Israel's side, they might blossom further from where the Old Testament enjoins a love for the alien and the stranger (Leviticus 19.33-34):

'When a foreigner resides among you in your land, do not ill-treat them. The foreigner residing among you must be treated as your native-born. Love them as yourself, for you were foreigners in Egypt. I am the LORD your God.'

From our viewpoint as Christians, praying for true peace is not an option, but a command:

Pray for the peace of Jerusalem:
   'May those who love you be secure.
May there be peace within your walls
   and security within your citadels.'
For the sake of my family and friends,
   I will say, 'Peace be within you.'
For the sake of the house of the LORD our God,
   I will seek your prosperity. (Ps. 122.6-9)

The Hebrew word *shalom* implies a state of blessing, well-being and reconciliation at the deepest level. However, true peace comes not through summit meetings, face-saving compromises and murky backroom deals, but through changed hearts. Ultimately, the cross remains the key. Through Jesus' death for both Jew and Palestinian the 'dividing wall of hostility' has already been taken away. There can be no lasting peace that bypasses the terrible price that Jesus paid, or its extraordinary consequences.

Indeed, it may well be that the Middle East will never enjoy real, lasting peace until Jesus returns. That does not mean that we should not strive for it now, but it is far more likely to be effective at the level of the human heart than with the duplicity and empty posturing of the negotiating table. Small-scale initiatives such as the Jerusalem Foundation[13] or the Olive Tree Reconciliation Fund[14] offer seeds of hope for a future where 'the lion will lie down with the lamb'.

Is a two-state solution the best way forward? On the issue of dividing the land it is all too easy to make unhelpful comments from the comfort of the sidelines. In praying for this issue it is vitally important to seek not what we want, what the UN wants, what the Palestinians want, what Israel wants, but what *God* wants. I know that many are passionate in seeking a two-state solution, where Israelis and Palestinians can settle down within securely agreed borders. These may both seem to be laudable and well-meaning objectives rooted in a real desire for compassion and justice. However, the warning to the nations in Joel 3.2 about the impending judgement that results from dividing the land of Israel should give us real pause for thought. Were those words only applicable in the distant past? Or should we be paying heed to them today?

Among a variety of ways in which the New Testament presents God as speaking to people is through the role of prophets within the church, part of whose role is to deliver messages which speak into specific contemporary situations. In Acts, for example, Agabus warns of a coming famine, and relief is organized on the basis of this (11.28-30). While I am aware that many today would no longer consider such practices to be valid within today's church, and would consider something spoken in God's name as shocking, presumptuous and even blasphemous, Paul warns us clearly not to quench the Spirit or to treat prophecies with contempt, but to test them all (1 Thess. 5.19-22).

For those who recognise the continuing validity of such prophetic utterances, therefore, I would like to draw attention to two contemporary instances, both given in Jerusalem in the first decade of this century, by David Noakes and the late Lance Lambert. I have reproduced these in part, the first specifically addressing Israel herself, and the second addressing the church. Although these prophecies, like any other, need to be weighed extremely carefully, the words do provide a further warning of the vital importance of seeking God's will in this matter, not our own:

January 2003, Jerusalem

Do not fear the conflict or the hardships. There will be shaking and upheaval and turmoil but I have warned you in advance in my Word that this will be so. In the battle set your eyes on me and remember that this is not your lasting home. ... Comfort yourselves with the knowledge of this truth and let your encouragement come from me alone. Do not fear the wars that

205

must yet come but rather *fear the peace that will finally result. It will not be my peace but a counterfeit peace inspired by the spirit of Babylon.*

Prepare my people for these days with the knowledge of my revealed truth. Teach them the whole Counsel of God and pray that they and many others will not be deceived in the time before the 'lamb of peace' is revealed in its true colours as the 'dragon of destruction'.

The strategy of the adversary is to wear down by continual attrition to the point where *in the weariness of conflict that desire for rest will make your people willing to accept a false peace which will prove in its working to be the deadliest weapon of all. Your nation will desire this peace and the world will desire to impose it upon you but do not be deceived.* Prepare my people to watch and pray and keep alert: strong in the knowledge of the whole revelation of my Word until I come, for only then will your nation receive true security.

April 2010, Jerusalem

Do not fear neither be dismayed for that which is coming upon the face of the earth, for I am with you, says The Lord. *Nevertheless I have a serious controversy with the nations. They are seeking to divide My Land says The Lord, the land that I covenanted to give to Abraham and to his seed after him through Isaac and Jacob, as an everlasting inheritance. This I will not allow without devastating judgment upon those nations who pursue this plan.* I have arisen with intense and furious anger and will not back down until I have destroyed their well-being. I will cause their economies to fail, and their financial system to break down, and even the climate to fail them! I will turn them upside down and inside out and they will not know what has hit them, whether they be superpowers or not. For I am the only One, the Almighty God and besides me there is none to compare. ...

I know your weakness and your tendency to fear, but do not be dismayed at these things. *In the midst of all this shaking, this turmoil and strife, there are two peoples that lie at its heart, the true and living church and Israel. I will use these matters, these events, to purify one and to save the other!* Do not fear, above the storms, the shaking, and the conflict: I am the Everlasting and Almighty One. In Me you cannot be shaken, you can only lose what is not worth holding!

How do you react on reading such words? Many will feel scepticism, suspicion or even anger. And if they were purely or even partly human opinions this would be a very legitimate reaction. But can we be certain that they are they simply the thoughts of men? Anyone with a modicum of fear of God would think very carefully before taking the dangerous step of clothing their own opinions as the words of the Almighty. For this reason, I would urge the reader to weigh and meditate on these words prayerfully as they stand before reaching a final conclusion on this matter. We can argue about theology and politics until we are blue in the face, but ultimately we cannot argue with God.

Finally I would like to reproduce an extract of a warning given to the United Kingdom by the late Derek Prince in June 2003. Asking why, despite intense and pervasive prayer, there are still no signs of a full-scale revival sweeping the land, he comments:

During the last half century, we have seen the catastrophic decline of both church and nation. As a nation, we have been stripped of our empire; all biblical standards of morality have been cast aside, while the church has accepted without protest or even applauded standards the world has set. In the light of scripture it is no coincidence that our national decline has run a parallel course to our unfavourable attitude to the nation of Israel. ...

In Genesis 12:3, God tells Abraham that those who bless his descendants will be blessed and those who curse them will themselves be cursed. In the context of the "Day of The Lord", God is much stronger in Isaiah 60:12, where He says unequivocally, "For the nation and kingdom which shall not serve you shall perish, and those nations shall be utterly ruined."

This verse should fill once again with considerable concern, all who believe the Word of God and take it seriously. In this statement, God confronts all nations with a stark choice; those who show favour to the nation of Israel will receive His favour and blessing, but those that will not will come to utter ruin and will perish. According to the clear word of scripture, therefore, any nation, including Britain, who will not serve Israel and treat her with favour will perish. ...

By embracing the teaching known as Replacement Theology, which declares that God's purposes for the nation of Israel have been superseded and cast aside ... we are corporately guilty of continuing the evil of anti-Semitism in our teaching, and consequently denying to the Hebrew nation the favour which God intends for her. ...

Will we repent and receive God's blessing and favour; or will we continue in both teaching and actions which deny the truth of the Word of God and fall under His curse? *The time for decision is now and if we do not soon repent, the die will be cast and it will be too late.*

Sobering though this warning appears to be, I do not want to end on a pessimistic note. However bleak the short-term future may seem, we should not lose hope. Although Israel may be at loggerheads not just with the Palestinians, but also with some of the Islamic nations which surround her, and on many occasions the entire weight of world opinion, the Old Testament assures us that this will not always be the case. Rather,

The law will go out from Zion,
    the word of the LORD from Jerusalem.
He will judge between the nations
    and will settle disputes for many peoples.
They will beat their swords into ploughshares
    and their spears into pruning hooks.
Nation will not take up sword against nation,
    nor will they train for war any more. (Is 2.3-4)

The LORD will make himself known to the Egyptians; and the Egyptians will know the LORD on that day, and will worship with sacrifice and burnt offering, and they will make vows to the LORD and perform them. The LORD will strike Egypt, striking and healing; they will return to the LORD, and he will listen to their supplications and heal them.

On that day there will be a highway from Egypt to Assyria, and the Assyrian will come into Egypt, and the Egyptian into Assyria, and the Egyptians will worship with the Assyrians.
On that day Israel will be the third with Egypt and Assyria, a blessing in the midst of the earth, whom the LORD of hosts has blessed, saying, "Blessed be Egypt my people, and Assyria the work of my hands, and Israel my heritage." (Is 19.23-25 NRSV)

For every round of seemingly futile peace conferences, round-table negotiations and two-state solutions, God's aim has all along been for something infinitely greater: 'one new humanity' joined together in Christ Jesus, who has broken every dividing wall in his body on the cross (Eph. 2.14-15). As we pray fervently for the peace of Jerusalem, as scripture enjoins us, let us ask for his perfect will to be done, not just in Israel and in the Palestinian territories, but across all the whole of the Middle East, and for the day to dawn where true *shalom* will touch every heart and mind across that very special but troubled part of the world.

# ENDNOTES

1   See https://lifewayresearch.com/2018/02/28/more-than-a-few-evangelicals-have-jewish-friends-and-family/

## Chapter One: The Wrong Bride?

1   This illustration was also employed by later Christian writers: Tertullian, for instance, draws on it in *Against the Jews* 1.3-5.

2   Andrew White, *Older Younger Brother: The Tragic Treatment of the Jews by the Christians* (self-published, 2014), pp. 4-5.

3   Derek C. White, *Replacement Theology* (Eastbourne: CFI, 1997), pp. 16-17.

4   Benjamin Shlomo Hamburger, *False Messiahs and their Opposers*, (B'nai Brak, Israel: Mechon Moreshet Ashkenaz, 1989), p. 19, translated by Michael L. Brown in *Our Hands are Stained with Blood: The Tragic Story of the "Church" and the Jewish People* (Shippensburg, PA: Destiny Image, 1990), pp. 89-90.

## Chapter Two: Massacre of the Innocents

1   Ignatius, *Epistle to the Magnesians*, 8.1, 10.3.

2   *Epistle of Barnabas*, 4.6-7.

3   *Epistle of Barnabas* 5.11.

4   Justin Martyr, *Dialogue with Trypho* 16.

5   Origen, *Against Celsus,* 4.22.

[6] Eusebius, *Life of Constantine*, 3.18.

[7] Letter to Theodosius in August 388, quoted in Jacob Marcus, *The Jew in the Medieval World: A Sourcebook, 315-1791,* (New York: JPS, 1938), p. 108.

[8] John Chrysostom, *Eight Orations Against Judaizing Christians* (387-388), 1.3.1, 1.4.2, 1.6.3, 1.6.4.

[9] Chrysostom, *op. cit.*, 1.4.1, 1.6.7.

[10] Ephrem the Syrian, *Carmina Nisibena* LXVII, 14-16.

[11] Hugh Montefiore, *On being a Jewish Christian: Its Blessings and its Problems* (London: Hodder and Stoughton, 1998), p. 25.

[12] Stefano Assemani, *Acta Sanctorium Martyrum Orientalium at Occidentalium*, Vol. 1 (Rome: Josephi Collini, 1748), p.105.

[13] Jacob Marcus, *The Jew in the Medieval World: A Sourcebook, 315-1791,* (New York: JPS, 1938)*,* p. 50.

[14] From *The Chronicles of Rabbi Eliezer Bar Nathan*, translated in Shlomo Eidelberg, *The Jews and the Crusader: the Hebrew Chronicles of the First and Second Crusades* (Hoboken: KTAV, 1996), pp. 79-93.

[15] August C. Krey, *The First Crusade: The Accounts of Eyewitnesses and Participants*, (Princeton: Princeton University Press, 1921), p. 55.

[16] *ibid.*, p. 261.

[17] Papal bull of July 15, 1205, quoted by Solomon Grayzel in *The Church and the Jews in the XIIIth Century* (New York: Hermon Press, 1966), pp. 114-16.

[18] Paul Johnson, *A History of the Jews*, (London: Weidenfield and Nicolson, 1987), p. 242.

[19] 'On The Jews and Their Lies', parts 11-13, in *Luther's Works, Volume 47*, translated by Martin H. Bertram, (Philadelphia: Fortress Press, 1971).

[20] John Calvin, *Ad quaestiones et objecta Judaei cuiusdam responsio* (A Response To Questions and Objections of a Certain Jew), in *Opera quae supersunt omnia*, Vol. 9 (Brunsvigae: C.A. Schwetschke, 1900), pp. 653–74.

[21] 'Jewish Massacre Denounced' in the *New York Times* (April 28, 1903), p. 6.

[22] Transcript of a meeting between Hitler and Berning, quoted by Martin Rhonheimer, 'The Holocaust: What Was Not Said' in the journal *First Things* (New York: Institute of Religion and Public Life, November 2003).

[23] Raul Hillberg, *The Destruction of European Jews* (New York: Holmes and Meier 1985), p. 7f.

[24] Kenneth Cracknell, 'Christian Theology after the Holocaust' in *The Way*, 1997 pp. 66-67.

[25] Rabbi Irving Greenberg in E. Fleischner (ed), *Auschwitz: Beginning of a New Era?* (New York: Ktav, 1977), p. 34.

# Chapter Three: Unbreakable Promises

[1] See http://www.astro.utu.fi/~cflynn/sand.html.

[2] See http://www.esa.int/Our_Activities/Space_Science/ Herschel/How_many_stars_are_there_in_the_Universe.

[3] David Lambourn, *But is he God?: A Fresh Look at the Identity of Jesus* (Milton Keynes: Paternoster 2014), p. 94.

[4] We can be quite certain that it is natural, physical Israel that is being described here. Early on in the chapter there are references to planting vineyards in Samaria (v. 5), and later there are rather precise geographical details about the rebuilding of parts of Jerusalem. If we compare the similar passage in Jeremiah 33.24-26 it becomes clear beyond doubt that God is indeed talking about hard-hearted, rebellious Israel herself, and that the promises are unbreakable.

## Chapter Four: The Spoiler

[1] Examples include Is. 26.17-18, 37. 3, 66.7-9; Jer. 4.31, 6.24, 13.21, 30.6; Hos. 13.13; Mic. 4.9-10.

[2] The account in Revelation goes on to relate how 'the woman fled into the wilderness to a place prepared for her by God, where she might be taken care of for 1,260 days' (12.6). Without wanting to strain the credulity of the reader further still, it is interesting that if we were to apply the day/year equivalence used in Numbers 14.34 and Ezekiel 4.5-6 to this passage (a similar system equating days to years appears later in 1 Maccabees and Jubilees) 1,260 years from the crucifixion of Christ in AD 30 would take us exactly to the first of the major expulsions of Jewry from Europe in 1290 AD, when the Jews were thrown out from England under King John. Although this may again be pure coincidence (and there are much more straightforward ways to explain the numbers in this passage) the possible correlation with the Biblical data at this point is striking. Once more, we need to ask the question, is there a hidden hand at work?

[3] Mark Twain: "Concerning the Jews", *Harper's Magazine*, September 1899, reprinted in in *The Complete Essays of Mark Twain* (New York: Doubleday 1963), p. 249.

[4] Leo Tolstoy, 'What is a Jew?', a privately published essay of 1891, reprinted in *Jewish World: an Illustrated Newspaper and Review* (London, 1908).

[5] A. B. Spurdle and T. Jenkins, 'The origins of the Lemba "Black Jews" of southern Africa: evidence from p12F2 and other Y-chromosome markers' in the *American Journal of Human Genetics* 59: 1126–33 (November 1996).

[6] The economics prize was first awarded in 1969.

[7] Source: http://jinfo.org/Nobel_Prizes.html.

[8] *ibid.*

[9] Source: http://www.jpost.com/Business/Business-Features/ Forbes-ranking-The-worlds-richest-Jews-310104.

[10] See, for example, John Walwoord, *The Blessed Hope and the Tribulation* (Grand Rapids MI: Zondervan, 1976), p. 134.

## Chapter Five: Reconsidering Matthew

[1] The Greek word for church, *ekklesia,* is used on a number of occasions in the Septuagint, the Greek translation of the Old Testament, to translate the Hebrew word *qahal (assembly),* particularly in Deuteronomy, Chronicles, Ezra, Nehemiah and Psalms.

[2] We will address this question further in Chapter 10, in relation to other passages such as Luke 21.24 and Acts 3.21.

[3] Philo, *The Special Laws,* 2.253.

## Chapter Six: Reconsidering Luke

[1] N.T. Wright, *Jesus and the Victory of God,* p.128.

[2] Similarly, when Luke quotes Paul's address to the Jews in Antioch in Pisidia, he states that it was only 'the people of Jerusalem and their rulers' who were responsible for handing

Jesus over to the Roman authorities (Acts 13.27) and that they were simply fulfilling 'all that was written about him' (v. 29).

[3] For more details, see Geza Vermez, *The Story of the Scrolls: the Miraculous Discovery and True Significance of the Dead Sea Scrolls,* (London: Penguin 2010), pp. 125, 132-33, 195.

# Chapter Seven: Reconsidering John

[1] It has been suggested, for example, that John wanted to sharpen the dividing line between Jews and Christians because of the so-called *fiscus Iudaicus* which was originally imposed on Jews by the Roman Emperor Vespasian in the aftermath of the First Roman-Jewish War of 66–73 AD. By clearly distinguishing themselves from Jews, Christians hoped to avoid paying the tax.

[2] See, for example, 2.466, 5.109-110, 6.71-79, 6.251-253.

[3] Talmud Sanhedrin 107b, Sotah 47a.

[4] *Corpus Inscriptionum Judaicarum,* Volume 2, no. 742.

[5] The expression *hoi pote Ioudaioi* has often been understood as Jews who had relinquished their faith: 'Jews who had acquired Greek citizenship at the price of repudiating their Jewish allegiance', according to E. Mary Smallwood, *The Jews Under Roman Rule: From Pompey to Diocletian: a Study in Political Relations* (Leiden: Brill, 1981), p. 507. An alternative explanation for 'those who say they are Jews and are not' is offered by William Campbell who suggests that they are 'Gentile Christian judaizers who, in order to escape persecution or for other reasons, called themselves Jews' ('Church as Israel, People of God' in the *Dictionary of the Later New Testament and its Developments* (IVP: Leicester, 1997, p.213).

[6] In doing so he may show himself to be less puritanical than those Christians who refuse to celebrate Christmas, and seizes

instead on a further opportunity to bring Jews to know about their Messiah.

## Chapter Eight: Reconsidering Paul

[1] Targum Jonathan Exodus 1.15; 7.10-12; Numbers 21.19, 22.2.

[2] Compare m.Nazir 6.7.

[3] In New Testament Greek the word *kai*, normally translated 'and', is often used in an epexegetic manner, meaning that it is used to define rather than to supplement the previous word or idea. If it was being used in this way here the NIV's omission of it would be quite justifiable. Because of a clear danger, however, of existing doctrinal presumptions shaping our understanding of the text, we should be wary about drawing firm conclusions about Paul's understanding of Israel from this verse.

[4] C. E. B. Cranfield, *A Critical and Exegetical Commentary on The Epistle to The Romans*, 2 vols. (Edinburgh: T & T Clark, 1979), vol. 2, p. 448.

## Chapter Nine: Sharing the Blessing

[1] It can of course be argued that Peter was writing primarily for Jewish Christians in the Diaspora (compare 1 Peter 1.1 with James 1.1), although this may not be consistent with his statement in 4.3.

[2] Karl Barth, *Church Dogmatics* (Edinburgh: T & T Clark, 1962), part 4.3, p. 877.

[3] It could be argued, for example, that the compromise hammered out in the apostolic decree of Acts 15 fell short of satisfying the aspirations of either side in the debate, but nevertheless enabled vital fellowship between Jews and Gentiles to continue within the church.

## Chapter Ten: A Glorious Future

[1] Letter sent to Baron Edward de Rothschild on November 2nd 1917, and published in the British press a week later.

[2] Martin Gilbert, *Churchill and the Jews: A Lifelong Friendship* (New York: Henry Holt and Company, 2007), p.112.

[3] E. P. Sanders, *Jesus and Judaism* (Philadelphia: Fortress, 1985), p. 103.

[4] Esther 4.14.

## Chapter Eleven: Israel and Ishmael

[1] Article 6 of the Hamas Charter (1988) vows 'to raise the banner of Allah over every inch of Palestine' while Article 15 states that 'the day that enemies usurp part of Muslim land, Jihad becomes the individual duty of every Muslim'. On August 17th 2012 the then president of Iran, Mahmoud Ahmadinejad, stated that 'the very existence of the Zionist regime is an insult to humankind and an affront to all world nations', and called upon 'all human communities to wipe out this scarlet letter, meaning the Zionist regime, from the forehead of humanity' (New York Times, 17 August 2012) .

[2] Ibn Kathir, *Al-Bidayah wa'l-Nihayah* (The Beginning and the End).

[3] A useful summary can be seen at http://www.judaism-islam.com/similarities-between-judaism-and-islam.

[4] Yusuf Ali translation; other Qur'an quotes are from the translation by Taqi Usmani (with proper names transliterated into their standard English equivalents).

[5] Muhammed Ibn Ismaiel al-Bukhari, *Sahih al-Bukhari: The Translation of the Meanings*, vol. 4, book 56, Muhammad M. Khan, trans. (Houston: Darussalam, 1997), no. 2925.

[6] *Encylopedia Judaica,* Volume 16 (Macmillan, New York, 1972), p.1532.

[7] Meir Abelson, *Palestine: The Original Sin* (Eastbourne, CFI Publications 2003), p.12.

[8] Pearlman, Moshe, *Mufti of Jerusalem: The Story of Haj Amin el Husseini* (London: Victor Gollancz, 1947), p.51.

[9] *Daily Telegraph*, March 19, 2002.

[10] Sammy Smooha, *Still Playing by the Rules: Index of Arab-Jewish Relations in Israel 2015*, p.34. at https://www.academia.edu/31576103/Still_Play_by_the_Rules_Index_of_Arab-Jewish_Relations_in_Israel_2015.

[11] David Lambourn, *op. cit.*, p.20-25.

## Chapter Twelve: Whose Land?

[1] Yusuf Ali translation

[2] See https://www.timesofisrael.com/bahrains-king-opposes-arab-boycott-of-israel-jewish-leader-says/.

[3] From a sermon on Sunday June 3, 1855, by C. H. Spurgeon at New Park Street Chapel, Southwark. http://www.romans45.org/spurgeon/sermons/0028.htm.

[4] From a speech given to the House of Commons on May 23rd 1939, quoted in Hansard, Series 5, Vol. 347, p. 2171-2172.

[5] Estimates of those who died in the massacre vary from around 100 to 250. The figure given here (supplemented by other corpses found lying in the streets), was that given by the International Red Cross representative Jacques de Reynier. See Stefan Brooks, 'Deir Yassin Massacre,' in Spencer C. Tucker, Priscilla Roberts (eds.) *The Encyclopedia of the Arab-Israeli Conflict: A Political, Social, and Military History*, (Santa Barbara: ABC-CLIO, 2008), p.297.

[6] A perceptive insider's view can be found at https://www.theatlantic.com/international/archive/2014/11/how-the-media-makes-the-israel-story/383262/.

[7] Geneva, October 16, 2009, in a UN Human Rights Council debate on the Goldstone Report.

[8] *A Land of Our Own: An Oral Autobiography* (New York: Putnam, 1973) edited by Marie Syrkin, p. 242.

[9] Rabbi Dr. David Friedman, 'The Political Reality of living in Israel, with a suggested path towards reconciliation,' first presented at a conference in 2006, and posted on the UMJC website.

[10] Andrew White, *op. cit.*, pp. 8, 45.

[11] Andrew White, *op. cit.*, p. 45.

[12] *Is Peace Possible? Understanding the Current Middle East Crisis* (Phoenix, AZ: Jewish Voice Ministries International, 2011), p. 54.

[13] For more information, see www.jerusalemfoundation.org.

[14] See www.olivetreefund.org.

# INDEX OF SCRIPTURES
(including both direct references and allusions)

## Exodus

| | |
|---|---|
| 2.1-10 | 76 |
| 3.7-14.31 | 17, 76 |
| 7.11 | 124 |
| 7.22 | 124 |
| 8.7 | 124 |
| 8.18-19 | 124 |
| 9.11 | 124 |
| 12.1-30 | 77 |
| 12.6-7 | 83 |
| 12.38 | 47 |
| 17.6 | 124 |
| 19.5-6 | 43, 139 |
| 20.1-21 | 76 |
| 32.1-29 | 76-7 |
| 32.7 | **113** |
| 32.32 | 124 |

## Leviticus

| | |
|---|---|
| 17.10 | 32 |
| 19.33-34 | **203** |
| 19.34 | 47 |
| 25.23 | 188 |
| 26.44-45 | **44** |

## Numbers

| | |
|---|---|
| 10.29-32 | 47 |
| 14.6-10 | 161 |
| 14.34 | 213 |
| 16.31-33 | 30 |
| 20.8-11 | 124 |
| 23.9 | 43 |
| 23.21 | 157 |
| 36.9 | 49 |

## Deuteronomy

| | |
|---|---|
| 4.6-8 | 46 |
| 7.6 | 139 |
| 9.27 | **44** |
| 10.17 | 188 |
| 28.37 | **53** |
| 28.49-50 | **53** |
| 28.65-67 | **53** |
| 29.4 | 100 |
| 30.6 | **123** |
| 34.9 | 161 |

## Joshua

| | |
|---|---|
| 5.13-14 | 188 |
| 7.24-25 | **108** |
| 13.12 | 108 |

## Judges

| | |
|---|---|
| 11.1-11 | 163 |

## Ruth

| | |
|---|---|
| 1.1-18 | 134 |
| 1.11-13 | 134, 148 |
| 1.14 | 148 |
| 1.16-17 | 47, **134**, 148 |
| 2.1-23 | 134-5 |
| 2.12 | 135 |
| 4.11 | 135 |
| 4.21-22 | 47, 135, 148-9 |

## 1 Samuel

| | |
|---|---|
| 1.6 | 19 |
| 1.10-11 | 19 |
| 2.1-10 | 92 |
| 2.26 | 92 |
| 3.18 | 92 |
| 4.22 | 92 |
| 15.9-26 | 201 |
| 22.2 | 161 |
| 27.1-12 | 203 |

**2 Samuel**

| | |
|---|---|
| 5.1-5 | 161 |
| 24.17 | 124 |

**1 Kings**

| | |
|---|---|
| 8.41-43 | 137 |
| 10.15 | 180 |
| 12.12-19 | 201 |
| 17.7-16 | 87 |

**2 Kings**

| | |
|---|---|
| 5.1-14 | 87 |
| 5.27 | 29 |

**2 Chronicles**

| | |
|---|---|
| 9.14 | 180 |
| 17.11 | 180 |
| 19.7 | 188 |
| 22.1 | 180 |
| 26.7 | 180 |

**Ezra**

| | |
|---|---|
| 1.2-4 | 150 |

**Nehemiah**

| | |
|---|---|
| 2.19 | 180 |
| 4.7 | 180 |
| 4.7-8 | 187 |
| 6.1 | 180 |

**Esther**

| | |
|---|---|
| 3.8 | 43, **60** |
| 4.14 | 162, 217 |
| 7.10 | 67 |

**Job**

| | |
|---|---|
| Book of | 63-64 |
| 1.1-2.10 | 53-4, 55 |
| 1.12 | 57 |
| 1.21 | 54 |
| 2.6 | 57 |
| 6.4 | 54 |
| 7.11-21 | 54 |
| 13.15 | 54 |
| 19.25-27 | 54 |
| 27.2 | 54 |
| 30.20-23 | 54 |
| 42.7-9 | 64 |
| 42.10 | 54 |

**Psalms**

| | |
|---|---|
| 2.8-9 | 55 |
| 78.15-20 | 124 |
| 83.3-8 | **169** |
| 94.14 | **44** |
| 102.12-16 | **65-66** |
| 105.8-11 | **190** |
| 105.41 | 124 |
| 120.5-6 | 180 |
| 122.6-9 | **203** |
| 145.10-13 | 157 |

**Song of Solomon**

| | |
|---|---|
| 4.8-12 | 7 |
| 5.1 | 7 |

**Isaiah**

| | |
|---|---|
| 2.2-3 | 155 |
| 2.3-4 | **209** |
| 2.4 | 155 |
| 5.1-7 | 71 |
| 6.10 | 99-100, 159 |
| 9.6 | 55 |

Printed in Great Britain
by Amazon